Privacy
vs.
Security

Other titles in the Issues in Focus *series:*

AIDS IN THE 21ST CENTURY
What You Should Know
ISBN 0-7660-1690-0

CENSORSHIP ON THE INTERNET
From Filters to Freedom of Speech
ISBN 0-7660-1946-2

CYBERWAR
Point. Click. Destroy.
ISBN 0-7660-1591-2

THE DEATH PENALTY
Debating Capital Punishment
ISBN 0-7660-1688-9

THE DEBATE OVER GENETICALLY
ENGINEERED FOOD
Healthy or Harmful?
ISBN 0-7660-1686-2

ENVIRONMENTAL TIME BOMB
Our Threatened Planet
ISBN 0-7660-1229-8

GENETIC ENGINEERING
Debating the Benefits
and Concerns
ISBN 0-7660-1587-4

GLOBAL WARMING
Understanding the Debate
ISBN 0-7660-1691-9

GUN CONTROL
The Pros and Cons
ISBN 0-7660-1673-0

HATE GROUPS
Revised Edition
ISBN 0-7660-1245-X

THE HUMAN GENOME PROJECT
What Does Decoding DNA
Mean for Us?
ISBN 0-7660-1685-4

HUMAN RIGHTS
Issues for a New Millennium
ISBN 0-7660-1689-7

INTERNET ISSUES
Pirates, Censors, and Cybersquatters
ISBN 0-7660-1687-0

KILLER SUPERBUGS
The Story of Drug-Resistant Diseases
ISBN 0-7660-1588-2

LAND MINES
100 Million Hidden Killers
ISBN 0-7660-1240-9

MEDICAL ETHICS
Life and Death Issues
ISBN 0-7660-1585-8

MEGAN'S LAW
Protection or Privacy
ISBN 0-7660-1586-6

NATIONAL PARKS IN CRISIS
Debating the Issues
ISBN 0-7660-1947-0

ORGAN AND TISSUE TRANSPLANTS
Medical Miracles and Challenges
ISBN 0-7660-1943-8

POVERTY IN AMERICA
Causes and Issues
ISBN 0-7660-1945-4

SAVVY SURFING ON
THE INTERNET
Searching and Evaluating
Web Sites
ISBN 0-7660-1590-4

TEEN RIGHTS
At Home, At School, Online
ISBN 0-7660-1242-5

TERRORISM
Political Violence at Home
and Abroad
ISBN 0-7660-1671-4

TV NEWS
Can It Be Trusted?
ISBN 0-7660-1942-X

Privacy vs. Security

Your Rights in Conflict

Ron Fridell

Enslow Publishers, Inc.

40 Industrial Road   PO Box 38
Box 398   Aldershot
Berkeley Heights, NJ 07922   Hants GU12 6BP
USA   UK
http://www.enslow.com

Library of Congress Cataloging-in-Publication Data

Fridell, Ron.
    Privacy vs. security : your rights in conflict / Ron Fridell.
        v. cm. — (Issues in focus)
    Includes bibliographical references and index.
    Contents: Privacy's widening scope — Watchers and listeners —
Searches and seizures — Intrusions and exposures — Students:
a special case — Privacy for sale — Privacy stolen — Privacy and
terrorism.
    ISBN 0-7660-2161-0 (hardcover)
    1. Privacy, Right of—United States—Juvenile literature.
[1. Privacy, Right of.] I. Title. II. Issues in focus (Hillside, N.J.)
KF1262.Z9F75 2004
342.7308'58—dc22
                              2003014755

Printed in the United States of America

10 9 8 7 6 5 4 3 2 1

To Our Readers: We have done our best to make sure all Internet
Addresses in this book were active and appropriate when we went to
press. However, the author and the publisher have no control over and
assume no liability for the material available on those Internet sites or
on other Web sites they may link to. Any comments or suggestions can
be sent by e-mail to comments@enslow.com or to the address on the
back cover.

Illustration Credits: AP/Wide World, pp. 26, 33, 43, 49, 55,
83, 96, 102; Corbis Images Royalty-Free, pp. 23, 37, 59, 68,
72; Corel Corp., p. 12; DíAMAR Interactive Corp., p. 90;
EyeWire Images, p. 87; National Archives and Records
Administration, p. 18; Rubberball Productions, p. 76; Skjold
Photographs, p. 63.

Cover Illustrations: PhotoDisc, Inc. (background); © 2002–2003
ArtToday, Inc. (inset).

Contents

Introduction 6

1 Privacy's Widening Scope 9

2 Watchers and Listeners 20

3 Searches and Seizures 30

4 Intrusions and Exposures 39

5 Students: A Special Case 51

6 Privacy for Sale 65

7 Privacy Stolen 78

8 Privacy and Terrorism 93

Chronology 108

Chapter Notes 113

Glossary 120

Further Reading 124

Internet Addresses 125

Index 126

Introduction

Sixteen-year-old Deborah Arnold is about to have a bad privacy day. It starts when a ringing phone pulls her up from a deep sleep. A telemarketer offers to sell her a psychic reading that will change her life forever.

"No, thank you," Deborah says. "Also, can you please put me on your do-not-call list?" Then she dresses and heads downstairs.

As always, her father is at the breakfast table reading the morning paper. The city has installed red-light cameras at five busy intersections, he tells her. The cameras snap pictures of cars that run red lights and the drivers get traffic tickets in the mail. Both Deborah's parents remind her to drive carefully. On the way to high school, Deborah sees an SUV run the light ahead of her. A bright flash comes from on top of the traffic signal. "Guess that guy didn't read the paper," she says.

She parks in the high school lot and hurries to the front doors. On the way in, she sets off the metal detector. A security guard pulls her aside and wands her and searches her backpack. Finally, the guard finds the problem. It was the silver barrette in Deborah's hair that set off the alarm.

Meanwhile, back home, Mrs. Arnold is feeding Deborah's baby brother when the doorbell rings. It is the installers from the wireless camera company.

By the time they finish their work and drive off, it is time for the baby's nap. As Mrs. Arnold puts Mikey in his crib, she smiles up at the new wireless camera mounted on the nursery room wall. In the kitchen, she watches Mikey on the portable TV monitor. He is sleeping soundly. She brings the monitor along to the living room. On the way, she glances into Deborah's room, where a second camera watches the scene.

Later that afternoon, Deborah must take a random drug test. That means urinating into a plastic cup in the girls' bathroom as the security guard stands outside the stall. Driving home, Deborah runs a red light. Shooting through the intersection, she sees the dreaded flash of the camera overhead.

Back home, Deborah finds her mail on her bed. She knows that one day soon it will bring her a traffic ticket. She throws out the junk mail unopened, all from people wanting to sell her things she never asked for. One envelope is welcome, though. It contains her new credit card. She had to cancel the old one when an identity thief used the number for an Internet shopping spree. The security chief at the card company suspects that black market hackers sold the thief her number, name, and address.

"At least that's over with," Deborah sighs.

She is all set to play her favorite video game when something new and strange catches her eye. A camera lens stares down at her from the wall. What goes on here? Out in the living room, her mother shows her the new closed-circuit TV monitor. There on the screen is Deborah's room—which doesn't feel so private anymore. Will her parents be watching to see if she is doing her homework and not playing video games?

* * *

Deborah is a fictional character, but events like the ones in her story happen to real people every day. They might be thought of as minor inconveniences—or something far more serious. Events like these are important to consider, because they have an impact on our privacy.

Most people desire privacy—they want to be let alone and to be in control of who knows what about them. Many people believe this to be a basic human need.

In the United States, privacy is also a right protected by law. If the individual who used Deborah's credit card number, name, and address were caught, he or she would be subject to punishment. But many things that can be considered invasions of privacy are perfectly legal. Some, such as telemarketing calls and junk mail, are made in the name of business. Others, such as drug tests and red-light camera photos, are made in the interest of public safety and security. This book is about these invasions, both legal and illegal, that affect our needs—and our rights—of privacy.

1

Privacy's Widening Scope

Some people enjoy lots of privacy. Others have very little. It can depend on where in the world you live. Citizens of nondemocratic nations often do not have guaranteed rights of privacy. Their rulers may control their private lives down to the tiniest detail. In Saudi Arabia, for instance, women must watch what they wear outside the home. If they fail to cover their hair, face, or ankles in public, they can be arrested.

In most democracies, however, citizens are guaranteed certain rights of privacy. In the United States, these protections were built into the Bill of Rights, the first ten amendments to the Constitution, which were added in 1791. U.S. courts recognize the Fourth Amendment as protecting citizens' right to privacy from government control.

The Fourth Amendment

The right of the people to be secure in their persons, houses, papers, and effects, against unreasonable searches and seizures shall not be violated, and no warrants shall issue, but upon probable cause, supported by oath or affirmation, and particularly describing the place to be searched, and the persons or things to be seized.

Widening Scope

Laws change through time—not necessarily the words themselves, but the way the courts interpret those words. The Fourth Amendment has not changed, but courts keep reinterpreting it, especially the part about "unreasonable searches and seizures." At first, only a person's house and possessions were protected. Government authorities could not search or seize them without a good reason.

Over the years, though, the courts reinterpreted this amendment and widened the scope of this protection. For example, in 1877 the courts added first-class letters and packages sent through the mail. Let's say that postal inspectors suspect that a package contains counterfeit money. Before 1877, they could inspect it right then and there. After 1877, they first had to demonstrate probable cause, a legal way of saying "good reason." They had to convince a judge that they had good reason to suspect that the contents were illegal before they could inspect the package.

The courts again widened the scope of privacy protection in 1891. That is when the Supreme Court handed down its decision in the case of *Union Pacific Railway Co.* v. *Botsford.* Clara Botsford was suing the railway for damages. She wanted money for an injury she suffered while working there. Railway officials refused to pay unless Botsford agreed to be examined by a doctor. During the exam, she would have to undress. Clara Botsford refused, claiming that undressing would violate her right to privacy.

The U.S. Supreme Court is the highest court in the land. It looks at certain cases only after they have gone through the lower courts. A lower court had ruled in Botsford's favor. Later, the railway asked the Supreme Court to reverse that ruling.

The Court refused. It agreed with the lower court and awarded Clara Botsford $10,000 in damages. The U.S. Supreme Court's decisions set new legal standards for the entire nation. In this historic decision, the Court stated:

> No right is held more sacred, or is more carefully guarded by the common law, than the right of every individual to the possession and control of his own person, free from all restraint or interference of others, unless by clear and unquestionable authority of law.[1]

Thanks to Clara Botsford, the right of privacy now included a person's actual physical self.

"The Right to Privacy"

A year before the *Botsford* decision, another historic document on privacy rights appeared. This was not a court decision, though. It was a magazine article. Two law professors wrote "The Right to Privacy" for the *Harvard Law Review*. They were Samuel D. Warren and Louis D. Brandeis. Brandeis would later become Chief Justice of the U.S. Supreme Court. Through the years, their 1890 article would have

The Supreme Court has heard many cases dealing with the issue of privacy.

more influence on privacy rights than any document since the Bill of Rights.

"The Right to Privacy" was full of righteous anger and concern. Its authors were outraged over what they saw as a menacing new assault on privacy rights. They put much of the blame on the snap camera, the world's first low-cost portable camera, introduced by inventor George Eastman in 1888.

Before the snap camera, subjects had to sit still for several seconds. If they moved, the photo would be a blur. Taking someone's picture in secret was all but impossible. Eastman's new technology had changed all this. Now you could take anyone's picture in an instant.

Warren and Brandeis were not concerned about ordinary snapshot takers, though. They were worried about newspaper reporters and photographers. Big-city newspapers were battling each other for readers. The all-seeing snap camera became a powerful new weapon in this battle. Were you newsworthy? Then someone might take your picture in secret. The next day, tens of thousands of people would see your image in the paper.

The Right to Be Let Alone

This might not seem like anything to get worked up about today, more than a hundred years after the snap camera's invention. In 1890, though, it could be a shocking experience. Especially upsetting were secret snapshots in newspaper stories about the personal lives of the rich and famous. Warren and Brandeis condemned these pictures as outrageous invasions of privacy. They wrote:

> Instantaneous photographs and newspaper enterprise have invaded the sacred precincts of private and domestic life; and numerous mechanical devices threaten to make good the prediction that "what is whispered in the closet shall be proclaimed from the house-tops."[2]

Their article asked the courts to widen the scope of privacy rights. The authors thought these rights should include any newspaper articles that showed people's private lives without their consent. Their plea was based on the "due process" clause, or part, of the Fourteenth Amendment. This clause states that no one should be deprived of "life, liberty, or property, without due process of law." They wrote:

> Gradually the scope of these legal rights broadened; and now the right to life has come to mean the right to enjoy life,—the right to be let alone; the right to liberty secures the exercise of extensive civil privileges; and the term 'property' has grown to comprise every form of possession—intangible, as well as tangible.[3]

In other words, a person was not just a physical, tangible body. A person also had intangible aspects, such as thoughts, feelings, and his or her image in a photograph. The entire person, both tangible and intangible, should enjoy the right to be let alone.

Zones of Privacy

The courts listened to Warren and Brandeis. Gradually, the scope of privacy widened to include more of these intangibles. One way it widened was through legal challenges. *Griswold* v. *Connecticut* and *Roe* v. *Wade* are two landmark examples. Let's see how the decisions in these U.S. Supreme Court cases widened the scope of privacy.

Griswold v. *Connecticut* took on a new intangible—the private sex lives of married couples. A doctor had been arrested and fined for violating a Connecticut law. Doctors and nurses could not counsel married couples about the use of birth control devices, the law said.

The doctor challenged this law and won. In 1965, the Court ruled that the Fourth Amendment created "zones of privacy" that should include the personal lives of married couples. Therefore, the government had no legal right to interfere in marital affairs.

Roe v. *Wade* dealt with this question: Was a woman free to decide for herself whether to terminate a pregnancy—to have an abortion? A Texas law said no. This law outlawed abortion unless it was needed to save the mother's life. *Roe* v. *Wade* challenged this law.

In 1973, the Court struck down the Texas law. Its ruling was based on the same "due process" clause of the Fourteenth Amendment that Warren and Brandeis cited in 1890. Since it was a U.S. Supreme Court ruling, it applied to the other forty-nine states as well. The zones of privacy now included a new intangible: a woman's right to decide for herself whether to terminate a pregnancy.

Tug-of-War

The framers of the Constitution knew that citizens must be guaranteed certain rights. Certain parts of their lives must be free from government interference. That is why the framers took care to build in limits to government power, such as Fourth Amendment search-and-seizure protections. They also knew that government would continue to challenge these limits, and this was good. A healthy democracy needs a constant push and pull between the power of individual citizens and the power of government.

So, as the scope of privacy rights widened, the government kept challenging those rights. Many challenges came during periods when the government felt threatened. One such period lasted from the 1950s through the mid-1970s. This was a time of great social and political unrest in the United States. During this time, private citizens and the government had an ongoing tug-of-war over privacy rights.

Communism and Civil Rights

Communism was one reason for this tug-of-war. Nations in Eastern Europe and Asia were adopting this totalitarian form of government, which many Americans saw as a serious threat to democracy. The divided country of Vietnam, in Southeast Asia, was one of these nations. In the mid-1960s, U.S. troops went to war against Communist-supported troops in Vietnam.

The Vietnam War put added pressure on U.S.

government agencies to watch for Communist spies at home. The Federal Bureau of Investigation (FBI) was one of these agencies. Thousands of Americans held public rallies challenging U.S. involvement in the Vietnam War. FBI agents watched these protestors, looking for spies.

Meanwhile, the civil rights movement was another pressure point. All through this period, people challenged the laws that kept African Americans segregated from whites. Gradually, these laws were struck down, but not without a struggle. This struggle included protest rallies and illegal acts of civil disobedience, such as sit-ins.

These civil rights activities also got the FBI's attention. Were civil rights activists organizing illegal activities? Were Vietnam War protestors secret Communist spies? To find out, FBI agents invaded the privacy of thousands of American citizens. They illegally tailed them, tapped their telephones, and monitored their mail. During this period, the FBI compiled secret files on more than thirteen thousand Americans, including scientist Albert Einstein and civil rights leader Martin Luther King, Jr.

News reporters finally exposed this secret surveillance campaign. Both private citizens and government officials were outraged. Congress responded by passing the Privacy Act of 1974. This series of laws established a special Congressional committee to monitor the Central Intelligence Agency (CIA) and FBI. The committee's job was to guarantee that these agencies did not spy on American citizens without good reasons.

The FBI sometimes violated the privacy rights of those who worked for civil rights for African Americans. This woman participated in the March on Washington for Jobs and Freedom in 1963.

Before the Privacy Act, the government was in command of the tug-of-war over privacy rights. After the Privacy Act, the individual citizen was in command.

Reversal

The events of September 11, 2001, reversed this trend. That is when nineteen Middle Eastern terrorists hijacked U.S. airliners and crashed them into the World Trade Center and the Pentagon. Congress responded by passing the Patriot Act of 2001. The Patriot Act gave the government back key powers that the Privacy Act had taken away. The FBI and CIA now had more freedom to look into the private lives of Americans.

Some people welcomed this reversal. They saw the Patriot Act as the correct response to a new kind of world in which terrorism posed a constant threat. If the American people had to part with some privacy rights to make the world safe again, then it was a price worth paying.

These new laws worried other people. They wondered: Would the government abuse its new powers? Would it turn from a friendly protector into a bossy Big Brother?

2

Watchers and Listeners

The name "Big Brother" shows up again and again when people discuss privacy issues. It comes from George Orwell's classic science fiction novel *1984*. Published in 1949, it tells of a future world in which a totalitarian government uses communications technologies to make people slaves.

If you lived in the world of Orwell's novel, your house would be equipped with a Telescreen. This is a wall-sized television that both sends and receives images. A dictator known as Big Brother uses this Telescreen to watch you, listen to you, and speak to you. He broadcasts instructions and warnings meant to keep everyone else in line. "Big Brother is watching you," he warns. In *1984*, privacy is entirely under government control.

Orwell meant the book as a warning. The way he saw it, democratic nations were in danger of becoming dictatorships. Orwell died in 1950. If he were alive today, he would see that democratic nations have remained democratic. Big Brother, the classic dictator, is not in control.

But what about Orwell's concerns with communications technologies? Are they really a threat to privacy? Warren and Brandeis issued similar warnings in "The Right to Privacy." If Orwell, Warren, and Brandeis were alive today, what would they think of video surveillance cameras?

Little Brothers

For most of the last century, you could easily remain anonymous in a big city. With so many people all around, you could easily melt into the crowd. This situation began changing in the 1990s, when video surveillance cameras started popping up all over. They showed up in apartment building lobbies, elevators, retail stores, banks—even schools.

How widespread were these surveillance cameras? In 1998, a group of people got together to find out. They were members of the American Civil Liberties Union (ACLU), a national organization dedicated to preserving individual rights and liberties. They surveyed Manhattan, in New York City, block by block, counting the surveillance cameras. They found 2,397 in all.

Video surveillance cameras were springing up in other big cities as well, and the trend continues today. Experts estimate that at least 2 million surveillance cameras are operating in the United States. That is roughly one for every 145 people.

If George Orwell were alive today, he might say, "I told you so." But it is not one Big Brother who is watching. It is many, many "little brothers." Of the nearly twenty-four hundred surveillance cameras in Manhattan, only about three hundred belonged to the government. The rest were owned by individuals, such as store owners, or by private organizations, such as banks and universities. Tom Colatosti heads a company that develops surveillance technology. He says,

> The average person is on a surveillance camera 30 times a day. When you go to a gas station, in an elevator, in a parking lot, shopping mall, ATM, Dunkin Donuts, 7-Eleven, highway—surveillance is a part of our everyday life.[1]

Extra Eyes and Ears

Why are all these "little brothers" out there? One reason is security. Surveillance cameras give law enforcement officials an extra set of eyes and ears—eyes that never blink and ears that always hear.

Sometimes these cameras help catch a thief. In 2000, the TV show *America's Most Wanted* broadcast images of several bank robberies in the New

Video surveillance cameras came into widespread use in the 1990s. Here security guards monitor video screens in an office building.

Orleans area, all committed by the same man. Surveillance tapes had caught the thief in action. In each case he wore a wig. One viewer recognized the "Wig Bandit" and called the New Orleans FBI office. Agents used the information to track down the suspect, who was later convicted of three bank robberies.

Sometimes the thief is a shoplifter. In the year 2002 alone, shoplifters made off with an estimated $31 billion in merchandise. In that same year, movie actress Winona Ryder tried to shoplift more than $5,500 in clothing from a department store in Beverly Hills, California. Security guards caught Ryder red-handed, but she insisted she was innocent. The store surveillance tapes helped convict her in court. She was sentenced to a period of probation.

Traffic Cameras

Another reason "little brothers" are out there is safety. Drivers who run red lights cause death and injury. Experts estimate that red-light runners cause some 800 deaths and 250,000 injuries each year. There are not enough police officers to catch all these violators. That is why some cities have installed surveillance cameras at stoplight intersections. These digital cameras photograph cars that speed through on red. They record the vehicle's rear license plate; the speed of the vehicle; and the date, time, and location. Police trace the license numbers and identify the owners, who then receive traffic tickets by mail.

In 1993, New York became the first city to install

red-light cameras. The city put up more than fifty at traffic trouble spots. Sensors under the road activated the camera just as the driver ran the light. These cameras were no secret. They were mounted high on fourteen-foot steel poles for everyone to see. They were there to catch violators, but they were also there to discourage people from running red lights.

New York's red-light cameras were well received. People agreed that the cameras did not violate privacy rights, since they started recording only after the driver violated a law.

When police made a similar move on the Hawaiian island of Oahu, though, they got a different reception. The Hawaii Transportation Department mounted surveillance cameras in vans. With the help of radar, the cameras took secret pictures of speeders' license plates. The program was introduced in January 2002. Just three months later it was cancelled due to a flood of protests from people concerned about privacy. Brent White is a Hawaii ACLU official. He said,

> If the government can put up these cameras to catch people going a couple miles per hour over the speed limit, what's to keep them from putting up similar cameras to catch people doing other things, like jaywalking?[2]

The Slippery Slope

White's objection was based on the "slippery slope" argument: Once authorities gain new powers, they almost always try to extend them. In other words,

Traffic cameras are used in many cities to enforce the law and improve safety. The digital cameras record the license plate numbers of cars that run red lights, and then traffic tickets are issued to the drivers.

once we start down the slippery slope, we keep slipping farther and farther down.

People use the slippery slope argument for different issues. Here, it is the right to privacy. The farther down the slope we slip, the more privacy we lose.

You will see the slippery slope argument elsewhere in this book. Citizens of a democracy have always been concerned with government interference in their private lives. Privacy advocates are especially concerned. Advocates are people who actively work for a cause. For example, there are advocates for saving the rain forests, eliminating racial prejudice, outlawing capital punishment—and preserving privacy rights.

On the other hand, the government also has its own legitimate privacy concerns. A democratic government is responsible for keeping citizens safe and secure. Government authorities cannot do this if they cannot get involved in the private lives of citizens to some extent. The issue is, to what extent should government authorities be involved in people's private lives? For example, should government authorities be free to eavesdrop on private conversations?

Carnivore

In the year 2000, privacy advocates exposed Carnivore, a secret FBI eavesdropping program. Agents were using Carnivore to secretly monitor e-mail messages, searching for evidence of criminal wrongdoing.

Agents could do this only with the cooperation of

ISPs, Internet service providers. ISPs provide computer servers for sending and receiving e-mail from home computers. An individual ISP serves thousands of customers. FBI agents installed Carnivore software to monitor all e-mail messages sent through an ISP's servers. ISPs could not tell their customers that the FBI was monitoring their e-mail.

Privacy advocates pointed out that Carnivore gives the FBI the power to monitor every e-mail message in the entire United States. Would the FBI abuse this power?

There would be no abuses, FBI officials said. The agency would be highly selective with Carnivore. They would monitor only the transmissions of people suspected of taking part in criminal activities. Carnivore existed strictly for reasons of security, not to spy on innocent people.

These assurances did not satisfy privacy advocates. They remained skeptical about Carnivore and the slippery slope of privacy rights.

Privacy Versus Security

Marc Rotenberg is executive director of the Electronic Privacy Information Center. He says,

> Now, as new technologies are deployed, one measure of freedom will be our ability to continue to move through public spaces and to spend time with friends and family members and others without the sense that we are being monitored by the government.[3]

Being secretly observed in public places bothers some people. Knowing the FBI can look at their e-mail makes them feel uneasy. These people have done nothing wrong. So why, they ask, must they be secretly watched and listened to? For those people, the quality of life suffers.

But what about people who fear becoming victims of criminals or terrorists? Surveillance cameras make these people feel safer and more secure. For these people, the quality of life improves.

So, what should we do with these "little brothers"? Do we remove them from department stores and ISPs and banks and schools? Or do we add even more? Do we allow the FBI to monitor e-mails for terrorist activity, or do we stop them? Either way, it is a trade-off between personal privacy on the one hand and public safety and security on the other.

3

Searches and Seizures

Being watched by security cameras is a small invasion of privacy compared with having police officers search your home and seize your possessions. Searches and seizures are serious invasions of privacy. Police may not conduct them without good reason.

For example, police may search a suspected drug dealer's house and seize any drugs or weapons. However, as the Fourth Amendment states, they must first show evidence of probable cause. A judge examines this evidence. If the judge agrees that it shows probable cause, a search warrant is issued. This is a written statement telling exactly what police intend to search and why. If the judge does not agree, police may not conduct the search.

Search of a Home

A warrant to search a person's home is a serious matter. U.S. Supreme Court Justice John Paul Stevens explained why in a 1980 Court decision:

> The Fourth Amendment protects the individual's privacy in a variety of settings. In none is the zone of privacy more clearly defined than when bounded by the unambiguous physical dimensions of an individual's home—a zone that finds its roots in clear and specific constitutional terms: "the right of the people to be secure in their . . . houses . . . shall not be violated."[1]

But is an individual's home truly bounded by "unambiguous physical dimensions," as Justice Stevens states? Normally, yes. But new technology keeps challenging the legal definition of *normal*. Can you search a person's home without stepping inside? Without even setting foot on the property?

Kyllo v. *United States* addressed these questions. The case began in 1992, when two federal agents pointed a hi-tech instrument at their target. The instrument was a thermal imaging device, and the target was the Florence, Oregon, townhouse of Danny Kyllo. The agents scanned Kyllo's townhouse from a car across the street. Their hi-tech device produced images based on heat energy from the target. The scan showed Kyllo's garage giving off more heat than the rest of the house.

The agents suspected that Kyllo was using heat lamps to grow marijuana illegally. The scan confirmed their suspicions. Based on this evidence, they got a search warrant and presented it to Kyllo before actually entering his home.

Inside, they found more than one hundred marijuana plants growing under high-intensity lamps in the garage. Kyllo was arrested, tried, and found guilty.

The Exclusionary Rule

Kyllo appealed the conviction. Appeals courts review trial court decisions to make sure they were fair and correct. In his appeal, Kyllo claimed that the agents violated his protection against unreasonable searches and seizures when they used the thermal imaging device.

The case made its way slowly through the court system, from one appeals court to another. Finally, nearly a decade later, it reached the nation's highest court. The U.S. Supreme Court announced its decision on *Kyllo* v. *United States* in June 2001.

Danny Kyllo won. A majority of the justices agreed that using a thermal imaging device amounted to an unreasonable search of Kyllo's home. Justice Antonin Scalia wrote the majority opinion. "The question we confront today is what limits there are upon this power of technology to shrink the realm of guaranteed privacy," he wrote.[2] The justices did not want that realm of guaranteed privacy to shrink, so they ruled in Kyllo's favor.

Kyllo escaped punishment under the exclusionary rule. This is a controversial part of Fourth Amendment privacy protections. It states that if authorities seize evidence illegally, that evidence cannot be used against a defendant. It must be excluded. In this case, the evidence was the marijuana. It was illegal for Kyllo to grow it, but it was also illegal for the agents to use the thermal imaging device when they seized it.

Search in a Public Place

What about a search conducted outside the home? Does the zone of guaranteed privacy include public

A police officer shows a visitor how a portable surveillance system can be monitored from a patrol car. Search and surveillance activities by police have been reviewed by the courts.

places? A Hawaii court took up this question. In February 1997, surveillance cameras captured pictures of Felix Augafa selling rock cocaine in front of a bar on Hotel Street in Honolulu. The cameras had caught him. The evidence was right there in black and white.

But Augafa claimed that the surveillance cameras had invaded his privacy. He said they violated his Fourth Amendment protection against unreasonable searches and seizures.

Danny Kyllo was in his own home when he committed his crime, but Augafa was out in public. That is why the court ruled against him. "The defendant cannot transform the 'public street' into a 'private sphere' by arguing that a right of expected privacy is invoked by his 'unilateral action' of engaging in a drug deal," the court ruled.[3]

In other words, the public street was not Augafa's home, so the cameras had not invaded his privacy. Augafa was convicted and sentenced to five months in jail, followed by five years of probation.

Warrantless Searches

The Augafa case showed that video surveillance in a public place was admissible. It could be used as evidence in court. The police need not get a search warrant before turning on the cameras. They may conduct warrantless searches in these instances as well:

- when evidence of a crime is already in plain view

- while police are pursuing a criminal

- in an airport as part of routine passenger screening

- in any public place, provided the officer asks in a nonthreatening manner and the person says yes

A warrantless search must meet one of these criteria to be used as evidence in court. Otherwise, any evidence police obtain in a warrantless search is excluded, as in the case of *Sibron* v. *New York*.

In *Sibron*, a police officer in New York City observed three men standing outside a restaurant one morning. He knew from past experience that they were heroin addicts. The officer saw nothing to suggest that the men were doing anything illegal. Nevertheless, he took one of them aside for questioning. This was Sibron. (In court documents, Sibron's first name is not mentioned.) The officer searched Sibron and found heroin in his pocket.

Sibron claimed the officer had searched him without probable cause, and so the heroin evidence should not be used against him. In its 1968 decision, the U.S. Supreme Court agreed. Chief Justice Earl Warren wrote:

> The police officer is not entitled to seize and search every person whom he sees on the street or of whom he makes inquiries. Before he places a hand on the person of a citizen in search of anything, he must have constitutionally adequate, reasonable grounds for doing so.[4]

Another warrantless search case had a different legal outcome. In February 1999, police officers boarded a Greyhound bus to conduct a random search for weapons and drugs. The officers had no warrant, so they could not force passengers to submit. However, they could ask them in a nonthreatening manner. If the passengers said no, the officers would have to back off. If they said yes, the officers could legally search them.

Two men who said yes were found to be concealing cocaine on their bodies. The men later said that the evidence should be excluded. It had been obtained by illegal search and seizure, they claimed, since the officers never told them that they had the right to say no.

The U.S. Supreme Court disagreed. In *U.S.* v. *Drayton*, June 2002, the justices allowed the search for two reasons. First, the police officers had not threatened the two men. Second, the officers did not have to inform them of their right to refuse. This warrantless search had not violated the two men's right to privacy.

Battle of the Books

When you buy a book, you probably do not expect law enforcement authorities to find out about it. You assume that your reading habits lie within the protective zone of privacy.

Officers of the Drug Enforcement Administration (DEA) challenged this assumption in 2002 when they entered the Tattered Cover bookstore in Denver, Colorado. They had found books about drugs in the home of suspected drug dealers. Now they wanted proof that the suspects had purchased the books. So they asked for records of customers' purchases.

The DEA officers had a search warrant. However, the Tattered Cover's owner, Joyce Meskis, refused to surrender her customer records. So the federal government took her to court. Daniel Recht, Meskis's attorney, said, "Book readers need to be confident that the government will not know what they buy and read." Meskis said,

> If these types of requests are allowed, there will be a distinct chilling effect felt as to the freedom of expression; otherwise I wouldn't be doing this. The debate within our government system as to right and wrong would be silenced, and that does not make for a healthy society.[5]

Many people would be surprised to learn that their choice of reading matter could be of interest to the government.

Meskis won the case. In April 2002, the Colorado Supreme Court ruled that the government had no right to know the books that an individual purchased.

Reinterpreting Rights

If those federal agents had been targeting terrorists in 2002 instead of drug dealers, Joyce Meskis would have had to turn over her records. That is because Congress passed the Patriot Act in October 2001. This series of laws widened authorities' search-and-seizure powers where terrorism was involved. Agents could demand to see reading records of anyone they suspected of having ties to terrorism. As long as agents produced a search warrant, booksellers had to obey.

The same thing was true for librarians. Some library officials protested. Here is what librarian Tom Geoffino of Fairfield, Connecticut, said:

> We're not just librarians, we're Americans, and we want to see the people who did this [the attacks of September 11, 2001] caught. But we also have a role in protecting the institution and the attitudes people have about it."[6]

Kari Hanson, a library director in a Chicago suburb, was more blunt: "It's nobody's business what you read."[7]

Meanwhile, government officials assured the public that the Patriot Act would be used only to gain information about suspected terrorists or spies. It would not be used to spy on ordinary people.

4

Intrusions and Exposures

In late nineteenth-century America, a new threat to privacy emerged. Author Henry James agreed. To dramatize this new threat, he created menacing newspaper reporter George P. Flack. Today "flack" is a negative label for a person who deals in publicity for a living. It comes from James's fictional character, who raves about "the light of the press." He promises to "set up the biggest lamp yet made and make it shine all over the place. We'll see who's private then."[1]

Freedom of the Press

More than one hundred years later, people still criticize members of the press for invading privacy. Despite its faults, though, a democracy must have a free press. The framers of the Constitution recognized this in the First Amendment of the Bill of Rights: "Congress shall make no law . . . abridging the freedom of speech, or of the press. . . ."

Journalists enjoy wide protection in privacy matters. Sometimes they stretch the boundaries of this protection. Few journalists have stretched them more than photographer Ron Gallela, who sold pictures to newspapers and magazines during the 1960s. Gallela specialized in taking hard-to-get photos of celebrities' private lives. He was known for tailing his subject and then taking them by surprise. At the exact moment they spotted him, he would quickly snap their picture. Often, the result was a dramatic image of a startled or enraged celebrity. This was fine with Gallela. The more dramatic the results, the more he was paid.

Many celebrities sued Gallela for invasion of privacy, but few won in court. No celebrity in the 1960s valued his privacy more than actor Marlon Brando. To demonstrate this, Brando once gave Gallela a broken jaw. But that did not stop Gallela from continuing to exercise his First Amendment rights and invade celebrities' privacy.

Privacy Torts

Most of these surveillance and search-and-seizure cases are matters of constitutional law. *U.S.* v. *Drayton* (in which the police searched Greyhound bus passengers) is an example. These cases pit the rights of the individual against the rights of the state or federal government. There are also legal cases that cover disputes between private individuals or organizations. These private, nongovernment disputes are known as torts. In a tort, a victim (the plaintiff) generally seeks money from a person or corporation (the defendant) who harmed him or her. The case of *Union Pacific Railway Co. v. Botsford* was a tort.

Torts of privacy come in several varieties. One is known as intrusion. The celebrities who sued Ron Gallela used the tort of intrusion, in which the plaintiff accuses the defendant of invading his or her privacy in a highly offensive way. Many intrusion cases involve the press, and the press generally wins them. This is especially true when reporters are trying to expose corruption, as in the following case.

Desnick v. *ABC*

The staff of the ABC-TV news magazine show *Prime Time Live* were told about suspicious medical practices at Desnick Eye Centers. Former patients claimed that doctors there had performed unnecessary operations on them. They had paid Desnick for expensive operations that did them no good.

ABC decided to conduct an undercover investigation of these claims. The network sent in reporters equipped with hidden cameras to pose as patients. The *Prime Time Live* report that aired on national television showed that the former patients were correct.

Desnick sued ABC for invasion of privacy. They

claimed that the reporters had invaded their space and eavesdropped on private conversations.

In a 1995 decision, an appeals court ruled against Desnick and in favor of ABC. Why? Desnick had placed ads in the media inviting people to come to their offices. So Desnick could not claim that ABC had invaded its privacy.

Ride-Alongs

What about intrusion cases where claims of corruption are not involved? Then courts are less likely to side with the press, especially when a private home is the space that is invaded.

Wilson v. *Layne* and *Hanlon* v. *Berger* are two cases that involve home invasion by the press. Since both cases tested the same legal principle, the U.S. Supreme Court decided them together.

Both cases involved ride-alongs to private homes. In ride-alongs, TV crews film law enforcement officers at work. In both cases, police officers served homeowners with search warrants while a TV crew filmed the action. In their May 1999 ruling in *Wilson* and *Hanlon*, the U.S. Supreme Court drew a "bright line" at the doorstep of private homes. A bright line ruling sets clear and definite boundaries. When these camera crews stepped over this bright line, they invaded homeowners' privacy. Chief Justice William Rehnquist wrote the majority opinion for the court:

> We hold that it is a violation of the Fourth Amendment for police to bring members of the media or other third parties into a home during the execution of a warrant when the presence of

News photographers sometimes seem to cross the line between people's right to privacy and the public's right to know.

the third parties in the home was not in aid of the execution of the warrant.[2]

Intrusion Upon Private Life

The press is not always the intruder. In the case that follows, the defendant is a major U.S. corporation, General Motors (GM), makers of Chevrolet, Pontiac, and Cadillac cars. The plaintiff is author Ralph Nader. Nader's 1965 best-selling book, *Unsafe at Any Speed: The Designed-In Dangers of the American Automobile*, severely criticized U.S. automakers, including GM. Nader claimed that by not making safer cars, automakers put millions of lives at risk.

GM fought back. They could not attack the book itself. Nader's facts about auto safety were clear and correct. So GM went after the author instead. They hired private detectives to tail Nader, to peek into his windows and eavesdrop on telephone calls. From all this, GM hoped to uncover and expose embarrassing facts about Nader's life.

GM's attempts to embarrass the author failed. Meanwhile, Nader discovered what GM was up to and sued them for invasion of privacy under the intrusion tort. GM executives and lawyers agreed that they probably would lose in court. So they publicly apologized and settled with Nader out of court.

Ralph Nader was a consumer advocate. His mission was to educate people about what is right and wrong with the products they purchase. The GM settlement of $425,000 was enough to fund his consumer-advocate projects for years to come. During those years, Nader helped create the Consumer Product Safety Commission and the Environmental Protection Agency, two federal agencies dedicated to educating and protecting the public.

Intrusion Upon the Dead

Everyone in a democracy is entitled to rights of privacy, even the dead. Thomas Condon, a professional photographer in Cincinnati, Ohio, learned this firsthand. Condon was hired to film an autopsy for use in training doctors. During the filming, he made friends with the coroner, Dr. Jonathan Tobias. Condon wanted to do something in the morgue that no one had ever done before, and Dr. Tobias let him.

What Condon did was uncover corpses and photograph them with props he had brought along. In one picture, he showed a female corpse with a large key resting on her opened mouth.

In January 2001, Condon made the mistake of taking the film to a photo shop. The technician who developed the film immediately called the police. Both Condon and Tobias were indicted and convicted of abuse of a corpse. Condon pleaded that his photos were art and so were protected by First Amendment freedom of speech rights. Judge Norbert Nadel disagreed: "They're not art. They're sick. They're disgusting. They're disrespectful and really the worst invasion of privacy."[3] Both men received prison terms.

Private Facts

Another kind of privacy tort is known as private facts. Like intrusion cases, private facts cases often involve the press. The defendant is accused of publishing facts that are true but are highly offensive and embarrassing to the plaintiff.

Private facts cases involve the First Amendment right of the press to freely publish news. Freedom of the press is not absolute. It must be balanced against an individual's right to privacy. Still, the press wins most private facts cases. This holds true in the case that follows, *Sipple* v. *Chronicle Publishing Co.*

In 1975 in San Francisco, a woman tried to

assassinate President Gerald Ford. At the last moment, a man in the crowd deflected her gun, saving the president's life. That man was Oliver Sipple, a Vietnam veteran who had won medals for bravery. In its story on the incident, the *San Francisco Chronicle* included this fact: Oliver Sipple was gay.

Sipple sued the *Chronicle* for invasion of privacy under the private facts tort. This law states that the facts under consideration must be newsworthy. Sipple claimed that the fact that he was homosexual had nothing to do with his saving the president's life. In addition, by revealing his sexual orientation to millions of people, the *Chronicle* had invaded his privacy and publicly embarrassed him.

In its defense, the *Chronicle* insisted that Sipple's homosexuality was newsworthy. Why? Because Sipple was well known in San Francisco's gay community as a campaigner for gay rights.

The trial court agreed with Sipple and awarded him cash compensation. The *Chronicle* appealed the decision to a higher court. In 1984, the California Court of Appeals decided in favor of the *Chronicle*. The court found that the story was a sincere attempt to "dispel the false public opinion that gays were timid, weak and unheroic figures."[4]

Video Voyeurs

In some privacy tort cases, the defendant is accused of secretly observing the plaintiff in a damaging or offensive manner. Perhaps the most offensive secret observer of all is the voyeur or Peeping Tom. The state of Indiana has the following legal definition of voyeurism:

> A person who peeps or goes upon another person's land with the intent to peep into another person's occupied dwelling commits voyeurism. 'Peep' means to look in a clandestine, surreptitious, prying, or secretive way.[5]

As we know, a person's home is the most highly protected privacy zone of all. Anyone found guilty of spying on people in their home can expect a fine, a jail sentence, or both.

On the other hand, people cannot expect to have their privacy protected in public. Privacy advocates say this fact should change. A chief reason is the advance of communications technologies. Hi-tech devices such as miniature wireless spycams leave people open to video voyeurs in public places.

Some states have passed laws to protect against video voyeurs in fitting rooms, restrooms, locker rooms, and other public places. In a 2002 case, a federal judge in Chicago ordered the defendants to pay more than $500 million to forty-six former college athletes. The offenders had used spycams to secretly tape the athletes undressing and showering in college locker rooms. The tapes were then sold in stores and on the Internet as pornography. One of the victims was a former champion wrestler. He said he saw the ruling as "a good win, as far as getting the sickness out of this world."[6]

Many states have not passed these kinds of laws, though. Barry Steinhardt, director of technology and liberty programs for the ACLU, said, "The technology is developing at the speed of light, but laws that protect our privacy are in the Stone Age."[7]

Home Watchers

The same spycams that video voyeurs use are used legally by homeowners and apartment dwellers. Some people have these spycams installed on brackets outside their windows looking down on their parking spot. A closed-circuit TV system records the scene. Homeowners say the sight of the camera looking down tends to scare off car thieves, and in the event of a burglary, the thieves will be captured on tape.

Some people use Internet spycams to watch their front door or store while on vacation. Wherever they are, they can check in from a personal computer hooked up to the Internet. If anything looks suspicious, they can phone the police.

Concerned parents use spycams to watch their children from TV monitors in their kitchen, living room, or bedroom. For small children, it is a matter of safety, with the camera trained on the infant's crib. For older children, it is a matter of discipline. Parents can watch the view provided by cameras mounted in their children's rooms. This way, they can see whether their children are doing their homework instead of listening to music or playing video games. Some parents monitor their children to make sure they are not using drugs or engaging in other dangerous behavior when the parents are out of the house. And some use hidden "nannycams" to make

Tiny cameras can be hidden in such items as a hat or a vase of flowers; the pictures they take can then be viewed on a personal computer or TV monitor. Some people use these to keep their homes safe or to watch their children.

sure that caregivers are not neglecting or abusing their children.

Internet Invaders

Privacy advocates worry about the Internet's potential for invading privacy. A case involving a Web site in Carrollton, Georgia, shows why. The site's operator, Neal Horsley, worked with Kenneth Scott, a photographer. Scott would wait outside abortion clinics to snap pictures of women approaching the entrance. Horsley would then post these pictures on his Web site.

Horsley and Scott were antiabortion activists. They were not invading women's privacy, they insisted. Instead, they were saving the lives of unborn children. By posting the pictures, they said, they were preventing other women from seeking abortions.

The women whose pictures were posted wanted no part of this public exposure. One filed a lawsuit against Horsley in 2000, accusing him of violating her privacy and subjecting her to humiliation. Horsley claimed that his actions were protected by First Amendment rights of free speech.

Whatever the trial court decides, the decision likely will be appealed, perhaps all the way to the U.S. Supreme Court. It will take many years to decide.

In the meantime, similar cases are almost certain to appear. As long as new communications technologies keep creating new threats to privacy, the clash between First Amendment rights of free speech and individual rights of privacy will continue.

5

Students: A Special Case

Young people have the same concerns about personal privacy as adults. They too want control over who searches their belongings and has access to their private information. However, students on school grounds do not enjoy quite the same privacy rights as adults. When it comes to rights of privacy on school grounds, students are a special case.

In Loco Parentis

Principals, vice principals, and teachers are responsible for acting in the place of a parent—*in loco parentis*—to make sure that students are safe and secure. How far should this protection go? When does it become an invasion of students' privacy?

Before 1969, these questions were seldom asked. Then came *Tinker* v. *Des Moines Independent School District*. This 1969 case was about freedom of speech, and it changed the way that the law viewed students. This was during the Vietnam War years, when many students objected to U.S. involvement in the war. Three Des Moines, Iowa, public school students, aged sixteen, fifteen, and thirteen, were suspended for wearing black armbands as a sign of protest.

The students did not think they should be punished for expressing their views in a democracy. So they challenged the suspension in the courts. The U.S. Supreme Court eventually heard the case, and sided with the students. In his majority opinion, Justice Abe Fortas wrote, "It can hardly be argued that either students or teachers shed their constitutional rights to freedom of speech or expression at the schoolhouse gate."[1]

New Jersey v. *T.L.O*

Tinker was the first U.S. Supreme Court case to officially declare that students on school grounds retained some constitutional rights. But what exactly were those rights? In later cases, the courts defined students' constitutional rights more clearly. One of these was a U.S. Supreme Court case from 1984, *New Jersey* v. *T.L.O.*

T.L.O. began when a New Jersey high school teacher caught two girls smoking in the girls' bathroom and took them to the vice principal. One girl admitted she had been smoking, and the vice principal gave her three days' suspension. But the other girl denied that she had smoked. Since she was a minor, the courts would refer to her by the anonymous label T.L.O.

The vice principal searched T.L.O.'s purse and found cigarettes, cigarette papers, a bag of marijuana, and an index card listing people to whom T.L.O. had sold marijuana cigarettes. The local prosecutor's office charged T.L.O. with delinquency for drug dealing, and she was suspended from school. T.L.O.'s parents challenged the charges in court.

As mentioned earlier, law officers usually need a search warrant based on probable cause to search someone. Did students on school grounds enjoy this right when it came to school authorities searching them?

On January 15, 1985, the U.S. Supreme Court handed down its ruling. The Court decided in favor of the vice principal and the school. But the important thing was not who won *T.L.O.* What really mattered was what the Court had to say about searches and seizures and student rights.

The Real Meaning of *T.L.O*

For the first time in legal history, the Court stated directly that students did have some rights of privacy on school grounds. School officials were not free to search a student anytime they wished. They did not need a search warrant, but they did need probable cause. The Court ruled that school officials could conduct a search only if they had "reasonable grounds for suspecting that the search will turn up evidence that the student has violated or is violating either the law or the rules of the school."[2] This became known as the standard of reasonable suspicion.

The *T.L.O.* ruling set another legal standard. The Court wrote:

> Such a search will be permissible in its scope when the measures adopted are reasonably related to the objectives of the search and are not excessively intrusive in light of the age and sex of the student and the nature of the infraction.[3]

This was the "reasonable in scope" standard.

As we know, U.S. Supreme Court rulings apply to every state. After *T.L.O.*, the "reasonable suspicion" and "reasonable in scope" standards applied to every school official in every school in the nation. For the first time in history, federal guidelines restricted school officials in regard to searches of students on school grounds.

Reasonable in Scope

The "reasonable in scope" standard generally protects students from strip searches. Exceptions are made in cases involving drugs. Generally, school officials can legally strip-search students if drugs are involved, as in the case that follows.

A teacher in an Ohio school noticed the odor of marijuana coming from a male student. Eventually, the principal and two security guards joined the teacher. Together, they searched the student's bag and jacket, then had him empty his pockets and patted him down. Finally, they had him remove his shoes and socks, lift his shirt, lower his pants, and pull his underwear tight. After all this, they had turned up no evidence of drugs.

The student and his parents sued the school, charging that the search was unreasonable and that it subjected the student to extreme embarrassment. An Ohio district court disagreed. In *Widener* v. *Frye*, 1992, the court ruled that the search met the

Many schools have instituted stronger measures to curb illegal activity and improve security. Here a student holds his possessions in a tray while a guard checks them with a metal detector.

"reasonable in scope" standard. The odor of marijuana justified a strip search, and the fact that the student felt embarrassed did not make the search unreasonable.

Reasonable Suspicion: No

In a Texas school, the vice principal saw a student behaving suspiciously. The vice principal suspected him of carrying drugs, so he questioned him and patted him down. When he found nothing, he asked the student whether he sold drugs, and the student answered, "Not on campus."[4]

A week later, the same student tried to leave school without permission. The vice principal caught him and searched his locker but found no evidence of drugs. The student's car was parked outside the school. The vice principal took him out to it and told him to open it up. The vice principal found marijuana in the trunk.

In 1992, a Texas court declared the search of the student's car to be unconstitutional. It violated the *T.L.O.* standard of reasonable suspicion. The car search was not reasonably related to the student's original infraction of trying to skip school. The student had done nothing that day to arouse suspicion of carrying drugs, so the vice principal had no good reason to search him. As a result, the marijuana found in the student's car fell under the exclusionary rule. It could not be used as evidence against him.

Reasonable Suspicion: Yes

By contrast, a similar Texas case had a different outcome. In 1997, police received a Crime Stopper's tip that a certain eighth-grade student had brought marijuana to school in her backpack. A police officer assigned to the school told the associate principal. Together, they searched the girl's backpack and found marijuana.

The student and her parents asked the court to dismiss the evidence. The marijuana in the backpack fell under the exclusionary rule, they claimed, since it was found on the basis of an anonymous tip.

The court refused. It ruled that the officer and associate principal had reasonable suspicion to conduct their search. The ruling noted that reasonable suspicion does not require as much hard information as probable cause. The anonymous tip had identified the girl by name and given her backpack as the location. This was sufficient for reasonable suspicion, the court ruled.

Lockers and Metal Detectors

Some students think of their locker as a home away from home. When it comes to privacy rights, though, a school locker is not a home. Courts seldom rule that school locker searches violate *T.L.O.* standards. This is especially true of schools that make locker searches official school policy.

Courts have also permitted schools to use metal detectors to search students. Searching students in schools is like searching passengers in airports. While these searches are not part of a criminal investigation, the courts still see them as reasonable.

However, school officials must be cautious when

it comes to searching students' belongings. They know that courts will not tolerate searches that deprive students of their constitutional rights. Any school official who violates a student's right to privacy can be prosecuted.

Student Records

Schools gather and record a vast amount of data about students. This includes grades, race, family members, family income, health, extracurricular activities, attendance, disciplinary actions such as suspensions, and any involvement with social service or law enforcement agencies.

This information raises two difficult questions: To whom should schools release this information, and how much should they release?

Federal guidelines help schools decide. These guidelines are contained in the Family Educational Rights and Privacy Act of 1974 (FERPA). They allow parents or guardians—and students, once they turn eighteen—to look at these records. If parents find misleading information or errors, they can demand a hearing to have the records corrected.

FERPA guidelines also make sure that students' privacy is protected. Schools may not release student information without parental consent, except in certain instances.

One exception is when a student's health or safety is threatened. Another is when a military recruiter or a higher education provider, such as a college or vocational training school, contacts a high

Though many students think of their lockers as private property, the courts have held that they may be searched in most circumstances.

school. Then the school must release students' names, addresses, and telephone numbers. Section 9528 of the No Child Left Behind Act of 2001 calls for this exception.

What are the consequences of violating FERPA or Section 9528? The vast majority of schools in the United States receive federal funds. If a school violates these guidelines, it may lose those federal funds.

Drug Testing

During the last two decades of the twentieth century, more and more people were tested for drugs.

Olympic athletes were tested for use of steroids and other performance-enhancing drugs. Federal job applicants were routinely tested for illegal drug use.

Eventually, students entered the drug-testing picture. At first, courts were reluctant to include them. In a 1988 case, a court ruled that schools could not require students to submit to blood and urine tests for drugs. These tests would violate their reasonable expectations of privacy.

But then came a landmark case in Oregon. Parents and school officials in the town of Veronia saw what they called a growing drug problem among young people. The prime offenders were high school athletes, they said. So the school district began a mandatory drug testing program for students who wanted to play school sports.

The program worked this way: Student athletes produced urine samples in the presence of an adult monitor of the same sex. For some students, this process was embarrassing. Boys had to stand at a urinal with their backs to the monitor. Girls used an enclosed stall, with the monitor standing just outside. Monitors listened for the normal sounds of urination. They had to make sure no one cheated and submitted someone else's urine. Anyone who tested positive had to take six weeks of drug counseling and submit to weekly testing. Anyone who refused could be suspended from school sports for two seasons.

These testing conditions left some students feeling like their privacy had been invaded. Others refused to take the tests at all. One student who refused decided to take the Veronia school district to court.

Acton v. *Veronia School district 47J*

In this case, an eighth-grade student wanted to play football. His parents asked school officials to let him play without the test. After all, there was no reason to believe their son was using drugs. When officials refused, the parents sued the school district. They claimed that this drug-testing policy violated their son's Fourth Amendment rights to protection from unreasonable searches and seizures.

This was in 1991. Four years later, the case had made its way through the lower courts. Then the U.S. Supreme Court agreed to hear it. The nine justices issued their decision in June 1995. By a 6–3 vote, the Court ruled in favor of the school district. Justice Antonin Scalia wrote the majority opinion. When it came to Fourth Amendment rights, he wrote, students were a special case. They could not expect as much privacy on school grounds as adults could. And student athletes could expect even less, since they changed clothes and showered together in locker rooms.

Like many U.S. Supreme Court rulings, *Veronia* was a split decision. One of the three justices who disagreed with the majority was Sandra Day O'Connor. She wrote a dissenting opinion telling why. The majority decision gave school officials the power to conduct an intrusive bodily search (the drug test) without probable cause, she wrote—a power forbidden by the search and seizure clause of the Fourth Amendment.

From *Veronia* to *Pottawatomie*

Veronia happened in the late 1980s. At that time, as now, drug use among young people was considered an extremely serious problem. The *Veronia* decision reflected this concern, which continued into the next century. A case from June 2002 showed this continuing concern. The case is *Board of Education of Independent School District No. 92 of Pottawatomie County et al.* v. *Earls et al.*

In this *Pottawatomie* case, the U.S. Supreme Court ruled that schools could give random drug tests to students involved in any extracurricular activities. Only athletes were tested in *Veronia*. Now school officials could order drug tests for students in band, chorus, the chess club, and the Future Homemakers of America.

Justice Clarence Thomas wrote the Court's majority opinion in *Pottawatomie*. It mentioned what the justices called a nationwide epidemic of drug use among schoolchildren. "We find that testing students who participate in extracurricular activities is a reasonably effective means of addressing the School District's legitimate concerns in preventing, deterring, and detecting drug use," Thomas wrote.[5]

Beyond *Pottawatomie*

Pottawatomie County is in Oklahoma. Other states also allowed random drug testing of students. One of these states was Indiana. At a Rushville, Indiana, high school, in 2002, drug-testing vans would come unannounced every few weeks to test urine samples

Schools can require drug testing for young people who participate in after-school activities such as sports, according to the Supreme Court.

from twenty-five students chosen at random. At Northwestern School in Kokomo, students attended a closed campus with video surveillance in the parking lots, locker searches conducted with drug-sniffing dogs, and random drug tests.

Were these Indiana schools known for having drug problems? No, but administrators made these policies to help provide a safe, secure place to learn at a time when, as they saw it, their students were at constant risk of becoming drug users.

School boards across the country are considering whether to have drug-testing programs of their own. Proposals range from voluntary testing to programs that make drug testing mandatory for all students.

Michael Lindley is superintendent of schools in New Buffalo, Michigan. He sees the student drug-testing dilemma this way:

> Some say it's invasive and you're assuming my child is guilty until proved otherwise. Others say if kids have nothing to hide, it's not invasive. We don't have a huge drug problem here but we don't want to have our heads in the sand.[6]

Meanwhile, privacy advocates see school drug-testing programs as invasive on the one hand and counterproductive on the other. They warn that as students lose their privacy, they also lose their respect for the authorities who took that privacy to protect them from harm.

Students are a special case when it comes to privacy rights. However, they face the same dilemma as adults: How much privacy must we give up in exchange for safety and security?

6

Privacy for Sale

The previous chapter focused on the right to be let alone. This chapter focuses on the other side of privacy—the right to control who knows what about you. Privacy expert Alan Westin defined this control factor when he wrote, "Privacy is the claim of individuals, groups, or institutions to determine when, how, and to what extent information about them is communicated to others."[1]

A hundred years ago, magazines and newspapers were the only mass media, and they seldom gave space to ordinary people. You would not expect to have facts about your private life made public unless

65

you were rich, famous, or notorious. Most people could control who knew what about them.

Today's electronic information age has changed all that. Personal computers, the Internet, and huge databases make detailed information about almost anyone easily available to everyone. This information includes official documents such as birth certificates, home mortgages, credit reports, and court records. These documents are all available on the Internet. And that is not all. Each day we add to this pool of information about ourselves.

Shopping Data

We give out information about ourselves every time we use a credit card at a store or over the Internet. Supermarkets are especially efficient at gathering this information. One of their tools is supermarket cards. Many supermarkets offer customers special cards to take advantage of special sale prices. These cards go by names such as preferred customer cards, shoppers' cards, and club cards. Your supermarket card gives you access to these bargains, but it also gives the supermarket access to your buying record. When you use a supermarket card, every item you purchase, from paper towels to potato chips, is listed in a database under your name.

Store owners have all this information collected into a consumer profile on each customer. These databases of consumer profiles then become products in themselves. Supermarkets and department stores sell them for profit. In 2002, one department store chain put the names of its 1.5 million credit-card holders up for sale at $90 per thousand names. For $15 more, the information came with the cardholder's age, income, and the ages of the cardholder's children.

Who buys this information? Direct marketing firms buy it. Then they contact consumers by the millions every day through direct mail and telemarketing calls, also known as junk mail and junk calls. The word "junk" is used because the calls and mail go out to vast numbers of people who have not asked for them and, for the most part, do not want them.

Direct Mail and Telemarketing

How vast? Direct mail firms send out more than 4 million tons of junk mail each year. That adds up to about twenty-eight pounds for every man, woman, and child in the United States each year. It takes one and a half trees per average family each year to provide all this paper.

While junk mail annoys some people, experts say that people find junk calls more annoying, since they interrupt private life at home. According to Private Citizen, Inc., a privacy support organization, 84 percent of the U.S. population dislikes getting calls from telemarketers.

How many calls do telemarketers make? According to the Federal Communications Commission, telemarketers place some 104 million calls each day to individuals and businesses. That is nearly 4 trillion calls annually, made by an estimated 4 million workers.

When you go shopping and use a credit card, information is used to build your consumer profile. Stores sell databases of their consumer profiles to direct marketing firms, who then target you as a customer.

How can the telemarketing industry make so many calls, hour after hour day after day nonstop? Do they have millions of people dialing every second? No, humans do not do the dialing. Automated dialing machines known as predictive dialers do. They dial numbers stored in computer databases. The computers keep close track of what each individual telemarketer is doing from moment to moment. When a potential customer answers the phone, the call is automatically transferred to a telemarketer waiting to make another call.

The Do-Not-Call List

These millions upon millions of calls get results. Telemarketers made nearly $300 billion in 2001. Each telemarketer calls on behalf of a specific business or nonprofit organization, trying to get people to buy something or make a donation. People may get calls from telemarketers trying to sell them almost anything, from a new roof on their house to a vacation on a cruise ship.

Telemarketers may initially contact anyone. But when someone says, "Put me on your do-not-call list," telemarketers must obey. After that, the business or nonprofit organization they represent may not call him or her again. Telemarketing companies that disobey may be prosecuted and fined by the Federal Trade Commission (FTC).

The FTC is a government agency that protects consumers from illegal business practices. For example, in November 2002, the agency took action against a well-known telemarketer. Miss Cleo's Psychic Hotline broadcast commercials on TV stations across the nation. These commercials urged viewers to phone psychics for valuable information about their personal lives. In return, the hotline would bill the caller at a rate of several dollars per minute.

Miss Cleo's also ran a telemarketing operation that became notorious for pestering consumers. Even after callers asked to be put on the hotline's do-not-call list, they would receive up to ten calls a day. As a result, the FTC fined Miss Cleo's Psychic Hotline $5 million, and the hotline's TV ads and telemarketing calls came to an abrupt end.

In 2003, Congress passed a law setting up a national do-not-call list. People could get on the list by registering by telephone or online at no charge. Getting on the list would keep most businesses from placing telemarketing calls to that phone. Charities, political organizations, surveys, and insurance companies were still free to call, however.

Registration for the national do-not-call list opened on June 27, 2003. The FTC estimated that 60 million phone numbers would be listed in the first year.[2] In September 2003, however, telemarketers filed suit to halt the program. The courts will have to decide whether the list will go into effect as planned.

Cookies and Spam

Lance Cottrell is a software company CEO who feels strongly about privacy rights. He says, "The Internet is more unfriendly to privacy than any communications medium ever invented."[3] Another software CEO, Scott McNealy of Sun Microsystems, also feels strongly about privacy rights. However, he says that consumers may as well stop worrying since, as he puts it, "You have zero privacy anyway. Get over it."[4]

In other words, because of the Internet, you can never fully control who knows what about you. Cottrell and McNealy are not exaggerating. Experts agree that more information about each and every American citizen will become easier to find on the Internet with each passing day.

Why? One big reason is cookies. These invisible tags are automatically downloaded to your computer every time you visit a Web page. Cookies allow Internet companies like Amazon.com to identify products that are likely to interest you, and then they recommend them to you when you visit their Web site.

Cookies alert advertisers to your interests in the same way. That is why you get spam, the ads that are sent to your e-mail address and that pop up over or under Web pages you visit. Let's say you visit several Web pages about taking tours to different countries. Soon you can expect to receive spam in your e-mail inbox from Internet travel sites that book flights, hotels, and vacation packages, thanks to cookies.

Stopping Spam

Spam is like junk mail. It is advertising sent to consumers who have not asked for it. How much spam is there on the Internet? An estimated 30 billion e-mail messages are sent each day. Of these 30 billion, roughly 10 billion are spam. And there is no do-not-call list where spammers are concerned.

Most of this data from public documents about you and Web sites you visit never completely disappears. It can always be retrieved, collected, and sold. Internet sites such as America Online and Lycos sell personal information and e-mail addresses of Web site visitors to mailing-list brokers, who sell it to advertisers, who pay professional spammers to send

Cookies are pieces of information that are downloaded to your computer whenever you visit a Web site. They alert advertisers and Internet companies to your interests.

advertising messages to each e-mail address. Professor Ann Bartow of the University of Southern California School of Law writes:

> We began shopping and chatting over the Internet. Shortly thereafter, we learned that anyone in cyberspace could ascertain our gender, ages, incomes, education levels, marital status, sizes, consumer purchase proclivities, aspects of our health, and employment histories, and the number, ages, and genders of our children, and that this information could be used to sell us goods and services.[5]

Your Other Self

Professor Bartow mentions personal information beyond shopping habits, such as education levels and employment histories. This information comes from public records. These records include birth certificates, driver's licenses, marriage certificates, employment records, credit reports, home mortgages, arrest records, court proceedings, and death certificates. They can be lawfully accessed by anyone, including telemarketing firms, private investigators, attorneys, law enforcement officials, and government agencies such as the Internal Revenue Service and the FBI.

Public records like these on every American citizen have always been available. But before computers, getting to them took time, effort, and money. Investigators had to visit different government buildings where records were stored, look through stacks of information to find what they needed, and pay to get copies.

Then personal computers and powerful databases became part of everyday life and everything changed. Now many of these records are stored on the Internet as public information. You can get them if know how; and if you do not, you can hire someone who does. Dozens of Internet information companies will gladly do the job for you. How much information is available about any one person? Ellen Alderman and Caroline Kennedy, authors of *The Right to Privacy*, write that the Internet is "like having another self living in a parallel dimension; it is a self you cannot see, but one that affects your life just the same."[6]

This "self you cannot see" is a computer profile of vital facts about you. It includes real estate or businesses or vehicles you own, newspaper articles about you, your current address and other addresses where you have lived, products you have purchased, medical records, and the names and phone numbers of relatives and neighbors. It is all out there for anyone to see.

Medical Facts

Of all the facts about people's lives, Americans tend to be most sensitive about their medical records, experts say. These records include information on any illnesses people have been treated for, both physical and mental. What if these records make people look like bad health risks? They fear that employers will refuse to hire them and health insurance providers will refuse to give them coverage.

These health worries are especially serious for celebrities and politicians. Nydia Velázquez is a case in point. In 1992, she won the New York State Democratic party's nomination for the U.S. House of Representatives. If she won the election, she would become the first Hispanic woman in history to win a seat in the House.

Her chances looked good until the day the *New York Post* received an anonymous fax from a hospital. Someone who obviously did not want Velázquez elected had got hold of medical records from a year earlier. The records showed that Velázquez had sought medical attention after an attempt to take her own life. "When I found out this information was being published in the newspaper and that I had no power to stop it, I felt violated," she said. "I trusted the system, and it failed me."[7]

This damaging leak of sensitive medical records might have turned voters against her. Instead, Velázquez went on to win election as representative in New York's 12th district, an office she still held as of 2003.

Secrets Shared

Why are medical records hard to keep secret? Because physicians, hospitals, pharmacists, and health insurance providers routinely share them. On a typical hospital visit, at least fifty different people may see a patient's records. Donna Shalala is a former secretary of Health and Human Services. She said,

> The days when our family doctor kept our records sealed away in a locked file cabinet are gone. Information about patients—their illnesses and medical test results, their medical histories, the drugs they have taken—is now stored electronically and transferred quickly from doctor to doctor or insurer to pharmacist. . . .[8]

This widespread sharing of medical records leads some people to shy away from getting medical treatment. For example, some women who would like to be tested for breast cancer don't dare go in for testing.

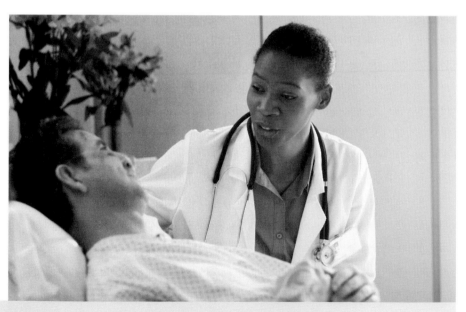

It is often difficult to keep people's medical information private. New federal regulations limit the amount of information that can be given out without the patient's consent.

Suppose they test positive? And suppose the results reach their employers or health insurance providers? They might be fired. They might be denied coverage. For the same reasons, people avoid getting medical treatment for depression or other forms of mental illness.

Lawmakers have wrestled with these privacy problems. Under the federal Health Insurance Portability and Accountability Act, or HIPAA, a new series of medical privacy rules went into effect in April 2003. They put limits on information that hospitals, doctors, pharmacists, and other health-care providers could give out without a patient's consent. These providers still may share information with one another and with health insurance companies. But they may not share it with the patient's employer or life-insurance provider, for example, without the patient's consent. Also, the new rules limit the information that providers may supply to marketers. In the past, health-care providers were free to sell the names and addresses of overweight patients to health clubs, for example. The new rules forbid them to give out this kind of information without the patient's consent. [9]

Privacy advocates said these new rules did not go far enough. They limited the release of unauthorized information, but they didn't stop it. Insurance companies still had free access to personal medical files. Privacy advocates went to work to strengthen these new privacy rules.

7

Privacy Stolen

People are free to gather personal information about you in order to sell you things. That is perfectly legal. However, they may not gather information in order to steal things in your name. That is a crime known as identity theft. The state of Texas defines identity theft as occurring when someone "possesses, transfers, or uses identifying information of another person without the other person's consent and with intent to harm or defraud another."[1]

Computer Crimes

That "identifying information" includes the victim's name, address, and Social

Security number. Armed with these key facts, the identity thief can successfully apply for new credit cards and go on shopping sprees in the victim's name.

How do identity thieves get this information? Before personal computers and the Internet, they had to go directly to victims and snatch their wallets or purses. Or they could comb through victims' trash for discarded bills and credit card receipts or preapproved credit card offers. Today's identity thieves can get this information without ever leaving their homes. They do not have to risk getting caught picking pockets or trespassing. All they need is a personal computer hooked up to the Internet.

The Justice Department says that some seven hundred thousand Americans are victims of identity thieves each year. In November 2002, federal agents broke up the largest identity theft ring to date, with an estimated thirty thousand victims. Some $3 million in illegal purchases were made in their name, all masterminded by a single perpetrator.

This mastermind worked for a computer software firm that supplied banks with credit reports. Every American has a credit report on file. It gives a detailed picture of a person's record of paying for items purchased on credit. Banks depend on these reports when they consider issuing people credit cards or granting them home or auto loans. If the credit report shows that the person made payments on time, the bank is likely to grant the loan.

The mastermind stole computer passwords that gained him access to thousands of these confidential reports, which include Social Security and bank account numbers. Then he and his two accomplices sold the reports to other identity thieves for $30 each.

Those thieves then used the stolen identities to set up illegal credit cards and go on buying sprees in the names of the victims. They spent as much as they could as fast as they could before moving on to a new victim. They also managed to withdraw money from some victims' bank accounts.

Long-Suffering Victims

Identity theft is a low-risk crime. Only about 2 percent of identity thieves are ever caught. One reason is time. Victims may not know their identity has been stolen until their next credit card bill arrives in the mail. By then, thieves may have run up thousands of dollars in charges, all billed to the cardholder.

Another reason is responsibility. Victims complain that police will not help. They say that police tell them they are not really victims. That is because cardholders are often responsible for paying only about $50 of the total amount stolen. Owners of the stores where the thieves went on their illegal shopping spree must pay the rest. These merchants lose billions of dollars annually to identity thieves.

But cardholders say that yes, they truly are victims. For one thing, their privacy has been seriously invaded. They feel used and abused. They want the thieves brought to justice. They are victims for another reason as well. The items illegally purchased in their name end up on their credit report, as items they never paid for, which gives them a bad credit rating. Without a good rating, it can be difficult, even impossible, to get credit cards and loans for cars and homes.

This bad credit rating is an error. The cardholder is not responsible for these nonpayments, but cardholders are responsible for getting these errors corrected. Three giant companies—Equifax, TransUnion, and Experian—maintain these reports. They have hundreds of millions of reports in their databases, and thousands of identity theft victims are trying to get errors corrected. That is why it can take months, even years, for victims to regain their good credit ratings. It takes the average identity theft victim 175 hours worth of phone calls and letters to restore his or her good credit rating. As privacy expert Stanton Gatewood said, "Once you're a victim, you need to be in for a long, long journey."[2]

National Identity Cards

How can we stop identity theft? One possible solution is to have the federal government issue each U.S. citizen an identity card. These national identity cards are already in use in Spain, Germany, France, and Denmark, where they have reduced identity theft.

These cards would include the kind of information that normally appears on a driver's license, such as a street address and photograph. In addition, the Social Security number would appear. But that is not all.

There would be another layer of biometric information stored on a computer chip and readable by a scanner. Biometric information identifies a person by unique physical features. On a national identity card, this could include fingerprints and a retinal scan—a record of the distinct markings on the eye, as unique as a fingerprint.

But do Americans really want a national identity card? Identity card advocates point out how the September 11, 2001, terrorists used false identities to enter the country, get training at U.S. flight schools, and board the passenger planes that they later turned into deadly missiles. Advocates say a national identity card system would have made those deadly events all but impossible.

Many privacy advocates disagree. Several privacy support groups sent President George W. Bush a letter speaking out against the card. Even if every U.S. citizen carried one, the letter said, "Terrorists and criminals will continue to be able to obtain—by legal and illegal means—the documents needed to get a government ID."[3]

The letter also claimed that a national identity system would actually make it easier to steal personal information. Why? Because this information would all be gathered together in a single document, which would then become the identity thieves' new target.

Privacy advocates also opposed the card because of who would issue it: the federal government. Government officials would then have all the vital information about every U.S. citizen in a single

Proposals for a national identity card include high-tech methods of identification, such as scanning the retina of the eye. Here the technology coordinator of a New Jersey school district demonstrates a retinal scanning system.

document, right there at their fingertips. A national identity card, they say, would bring us a giant step closer to a Big Brother society.

Shortly after the events of September 11, 2001, surveys showed that more than two thirds of the American people favored a national identity system. But by March 2002, that number had dropped to just 26 percent. The Bush administration agreed. It had no interest in such a system.

Stalking

Stalkers are not identity thieves, but they also use personal information to victimize people—sometimes fatally. Most stalkers are men, and most of their targets are women with whom they are obsessed. To be obsessed is to be so focused on someone that nothing else matters. You must get to this person no matter what.

Television and movie actress Rebecca Schaeffer was the target of one obsessed stalker. In 1989 he hired a private detective to find her unlisted home address. The job was easy. The detective simply got in touch with the California Department of Motor Vehicles, which promptly gave him Schaeffer's address, no questions asked.

Armed with this information, the stalker disguised himself as a flower delivery man and gained entry to Rebecca Schaeffer's house. There, he shot her to death.

Since this killing involved a celebrity, it got lots of media coverage, which helped push Congress to make new laws. In 1994, Congress passed the Driver's Privacy Protection Act, which restricted the information that state motor vehicle facilities could release to the public.

Internet Contacts

Unfortunately, lawmakers have done little to restrict identity thieves and stalkers from getting personal information off the Internet. Let's look at the case of Michael Campbell. He was eighteen when he became obsessed with the shooting rampage at Columbine High School in Colorado in April 1999. That is when two students shot and killed twelve students and a teacher before taking their own lives.

In December 1999, Campbell went looking for a Columbine student on the Internet. Using America Online's instant messaging system, he made anonymous contact with a sixteen-year-old Columbine student. Using his Internet handle, Soup81, Campbell sent the student a chilling message. He wrote that he would finish what the Columbine shooters had started.

FBI agents obtained a search warrant and tracked the source of the message back through Campbell's ISP to his computer. In January 2000, Michael Campbell was found guilty of threatening the student and was sentenced to four months in prison and three years' probation.

Privacy experts and law enforcement authorities point to this and similar cases when they urge caution in regard to Internet contact. Revealing your real name and address to anyone you "meet" over the Internet, whether it is through a messaging system or a chat room, could put you in contact with an identity thief or stalker.

Deception

One strategy of privacy invaders sounds more like fiction than fact. It is known as pretexting. A pretext is a false reason used to conceal the real reason for getting or doing something. Pretexters, the people who do it, are usually private investigators out to get private information about someone for a client.

Let's call that someone the subject. The pretexter contacts the subject's friends, coworkers, and family members under a pretext of some kind. Often, the pretexter claims to have money for the subject. In this way, pretexters get people to give them the information they seek.

Pretexting can prove fatal for the subject. In October 1999, Liam Youens contacted Docusearch, a company specializing in getting private information. Youens wanted the work address of Amy Boyer. Docusearch did not ask Youens why he wanted this information. They did not know that he was obsessed with Amy Boyer and out to kill her.

Docusearch put investigator Michele Gambino on the job. She called Boyer's mother, pretending to be an official from an insurance company with a cash refund for Amy. Mrs. Boyer fell for this pretext and gave Amy's address to Gambino, who then gave it to her client. A few days later, in front of her workplace, Youens shot Amy Boyer to death.

Neither Gambino nor anyone else connected with Docusearch suspected that their client was out to do harm. However, Docusearch owner Daniel Cohn admitted that identity thieves do sometimes use the company to help them commit crimes. Another Docusearch investigator, Matthew Cloth, said that the practice of pretexting "has exploded within the last five years. It's totally out of control."[4]

Theft of private information is growing all the time. Identity thieves, terrorists, and stalkers are getting

Unfortunately, it is easy for thieves and stalkers to gather personal information from the Internet. Young users may put themselves in danger when they use instant messaging or visit chat rooms.

more and more skillful at secretly invading people's privacy. Lawmakers and police try to protect people from these criminal invaders, but there are also things that people can do to protect themselves.

Protecting Your Privacy

The FTC publishes advice on how to help keep your personal information private. This passage from an FTC document explains how the electronic information age has affected personal privacy, both for good and bad. First, the good news:

> Advances in computer technology have made it possible for detailed information about people to be compiled and shared more easily and cheaply than ever. That has produced many benefits for society as a whole and individual consumers. For example, it is easier for law enforcement to track down criminals, for banks to prevent fraud, and for consumers to learn about new products and services, allowing them to make better-informed purchasing decisions.

> Now, the bad news.

> At the same time, as personal information becomes more accessible, each of us—companies, associations, government agencies, and consumers—must take precautions to protect against the misuse of our information.[5]

Privacy advocates agree. There are not enough laws in place to protect us, and with the constant advance of electronic technologies, there may never be. So it is up to each of us to protect our own privacy. How can we do this?

Social Security Numbers

Your Social Security number is the single most important piece of infomation about you. No other form of identification plays a more important part in establishing personal identity.

On the other hand, no other form of identification poses a greater risk to personal privacy. Stealing your Social Security number is an identity thief's number-one goal. Here are some warnings from privacy experts about guarding your Social Security number:

- Do not give out your number unless you have to. For example, you must give it out to get a job or open a bank account but not to apply for a credit card or insurance policy.

- Do not carry your Social Security card in your purse or wallet, where thieves might get at it.

- Be careful about documents you throw away. A bank statement, for instance, may list the owner's Social Security number. This also goes for preapproved credit card applications that come through the mail. Any document with your Social Security number on it should be torn up or shredded before you throw it away.

Privacy Warnings

Privacy experts issue these warnings about guarding other pieces of personal information:

- Never give out personal information over the telephone to an unfamiliar person or company.

This includes your credit card number, bank account number, home address, phone number, mother's maiden name, and any personal medical information.

- Think twice before filling out application forms or warranties for products you have bought, such as computers, cameras, or stereo equipment. The company that sold you the product may sell this information to advertisers, and that will increase your junk mail.

- Use these same precautions when you shop on the Internet. Think carefully before filling

Giving out credit card information over the phone or the Internet can be risky. Shoppers should exercise caution about the information they share.

out online questionnaires and surveys. The completed forms may lead to an avalanche of spam.

- You can help stop banks, credit card companies, and merchants from selling your personal information to advertisers. Write them a letter stating, "I want to opt out of information sharing to the maximum extent permitted by law."

- If you do not want to speak with telemarketers, you may simply hang up. But then they may invade your privacy again at a later date. By law, however, they are not allowed to call back again if you tell them, "Put me on your do-not-call list." Breaking this law can lead to harsh penalties.

- Conduct an Internet search on yourself. Type your name in on a search engine such as Google or Yahoo. The results might surprise you. You might see personal information that you had no idea was out there. If you want it removed, contact the Webmaster or the owner of the site.

- Finally, remember to be careful what you write whenever you send an e-mail. E-mail messages are never really private. The receiver could instantly pass them on to anyone anywhere.

This last warning goes for anyone with a personal computer. It is especially important for employees who work in offices and for college students. Employers have the legal right to monitor any e-mail their employees send from computers used in their business. People have been caught and disciplined for sending uncomplimentary e-mails about their bosses or for sending e-mails that are unrelated to work.

College students must be cautious for the same reason. Colleges can install software to legally monitor any e-mails sent through their servers. Remember: Nothing you send over the Internet is ever truly private.

8

Privacy and Terrorism

After the terrorist attacks on September 11, 2001, Americans knew their daily lives would change. Stewart A. Baker, a former National Security Agency official, said: "It's the end of a nice, comfortable set of assumptions that allowed us to keep ourselves protected from some kinds of intrusions."[1]

Suddenly Americans saw their free and open society in a menacing new light. If democracy meant freedom for anyone, then it meant freedom for terrorists too. These shadowy figures could be anywhere. They could strike at any time. How could Americans continue to live freely and openly in such a dangerous world? What changes must they make to deal with this terrorist threat?

Conflicting Concerns

After 9-11, concerns about freedom versus security sparked national debate. For some people, the foremost concern was security. There was a war on, the war on terrorism. To protect citizens in time of war, the government must have expanded powers. Like it or not, Americans must surrender some freedoms for the greater good of protection from terrorists.

Some of these freedoms involved privacy. Robert Pitofsky, former head of the FTC, said, "Terrorists swim in a society in which privacy is protected. If some invasions of privacy are necessary to bring them out into the open, most people are going to say, 'OK, go ahead.'"[2] Mary Jo White, who has prosecuted terrorists in New York City, agrees: "We're now at war. The public safety concern has to come first. Would that we wouldn't have to pay this price for our own safety and national security. But we do."[3]

For other people, the first and foremost concern was freedom. They wondered, would the 9-11 attacks lead to an attack on Americans' rights to privacy? Yes, we had to fight terrorism. But what if we went too far? What if we gave up too many freedoms in the name of security? What if one of these freedoms was the right to privacy? Would we wake up one day to find Big Brother in charge of our private lives?

The Patriot Act of 2001

The American people's early reaction to the 9-11 attacks could be summed up in five words: Let's do whatever it takes. They were ready to grant the government sweeping new powers to track down terrorists. Lawmakers responded quickly. By a vote of 98–1 in the Senate and 357–66 in the House of Representatives, Congress passed the Patriot Act of October 2001.

The act amended fifteen existing federal laws. Some amendments gave the FBI new powers where terrorism was involved. For example, when agents demanded customer records of terrorist suspects, merchants and librarians had to turn them over. Agents were now free to monitor a suspected terrorist's e-mails and telephone calls. They could also keep track of who attended political rallies and religious services. Before agents could exercise these new powers, however, they still had to get warrants from judges. But they no longer had to supply judges with evidence of probable cause if terrorism was involved.

How would these new powers help law enforcement authorities fight terrorism? David Cohen, a former federal intelligence official, explained:

> We have seen how the mosque and Islamic institutes have been used to shield the work of terrorists from law enforcement scrutiny by taking advantage of restrictions on the investigation of First Amendment activity.[4]

In other words, terrorists had misused protections

Following the terrorist attacks on the World Trade Center and the Pentagon on September 11, 2001, some Americans felt that security concerns outweighed the issues of privacy and freedom. Shown are firemen working amid the wreckage of the Twin Towers.

guaranteed by the Bill of Rights, such as freedom of religion and protection from illegal searches and seizures. They had used those protections to hide their criminal activities. Now agents could use these new powers to help them find terrorists.

When privacy advocates looked at the Patriot Act, though, they were skeptical. They thought of the Vietnam War and civil rights era, when the FBI and CIA spied on thousands of innocent people. ACLU official Laura Murphy said, "This is not a direct response to terrorism. This is part of a long-standing FBI wish list for unfettered investigative powers."[5]

FBI director Robert Mueller was quick to assure that nothing like what happened back then would happen now. "We need to rigorously conform to constitutional and statutory protections in the conduct of our investigations," Mueller said. "And under these revised guidelines we will continue to do so."[6]

The Department of Homeland Security

Mueller's assurances did not assure everyone. Privacy advocates worried about new government moves to fight terrorism. One of these moves was the creation of the Department of Homeland Security (DHS) in January 2002. Under the DHS, twenty-two separate government agencies were now brought together into a single department. These agencies included the FBI, the Coast Guard, and the Immigration and Naturalization Service. DHS officials explained the department's purpose: "Component agencies will analyze threats and intelligence, guard our borders and airports, protect our critical infrastructure, and coordinate the response of our nation for future emergencies."[7]

Privacy advocates were concerned about power. Now the combined powers of twenty-two government agencies belonged to a single department. They were also concerned about information. Along with these combined powers came the combined database information that these agencies held on American citizens. All this power and information in one place—was this wise? Could the DHS turn into Big Brother someday?

DHS head Tom Ridge assured the public that the DHS would be a threat to terrorists only. "The Department of Homeland Security will have a single mission," he said. "As the President reminds all of us, it is his most important job, and the most important job of the federal government: protect the American people and our way of life from terrorism."[8]

Operation TIPS

Privacy advocates saw a new concern in July 2002. That was when Attorney General John Ashcroft announced a new national surveillance initiative called Operation TIPS (Terrorist Information and Prevention System). TIPS was a national surveillance system designed to give everyone a chance to fight terrorism. Ashcroft wanted all American citizens to be on the lookout and report any suspicious activities to authorities.

Ashcroft singled out truck and bus drivers, meter

readers, and letter carriers. Their work put them in good positions to see what people were doing on the street and in their businesses and homes. Of course, they could not legally enter private homes where they detected suspicious activities, Ashcroft said. Instead, they should report their suspicions to police or the FBI.

Some citizens welcomed the announcement. They had been looking out for terrorists even before Operation TIPS. Richard Rucireto was a Federal Express delivery truck driver in Brooklyn, New York. Ever since the 9-11 attacks, he had been keeping a close watch on his Arab-American customers. "Whenever I would go to a place where there was a lot of them, I would tell the landlord, hey, you got nine people living up there or whatever, and they would call the FBI and get them checked out."[9]

Ashcroft's program was based on good intentions: to fight terrorism. However, the idea of having citizens in a democracy spy on one another sparked stiff opposition. Lawmakers in both houses of Congress spoke out against TIPS. Dick Armey was the House majority leader. He said, "Citizens should not be spying on each other."[10] And Senator Orrin Hatch of Utah said, "We don't want to see a *1984* Orwellian-type situation here where neighbors are reporting on neighbors."[11]

Soon after announcing Operation TIPS, Ashcroft eliminated it. He realized that even in light of the terrorist attacks, Americans were not prepared to spy on one another.

Airport Searches

After the 9-11 attacks, many Americans demanded stronger airport security. But when new, stiffer regulations were put into effect early in 2002, privacy problems came with them. Anyone flying during the first half of 2002 noticed the changes, and some passengers did not like what they saw.

In March 2002, a family was flying back home to Pittsburgh, Pennsylvania, after an Orlando, Florida, vacation. As the family was about to board, a gate agent pulled aside the three-year-old daughter. The parents complained. The agent said yes, he knew she was only three years old. However, she would still have to be wanded and searched. Why? The agent gave no reason, and the search proceeded.

Then there was Joe Foss, the eighty-six-year-old retired Marine Corps general on his way to West Point, the U.S. military academy in New York. He was scheduled to speak to cadets about his World War II flying experiences. The school had asked him to bring along his Medal of Honor.

The Medal of Honor is awarded to soldiers who showed extreme bravery in defending America in wartime. When they noticed it, security screeners at Sky Harbor International Airport in Phoenix, Arizona, pulled the general aside. The general's medal reminded them of the box cutters that the 9-11 terrorists had used to hijack the three airliners. Since it was star-shaped, the screeners decided, the Medal of Honor could be used as a weapon. The screeners wanted to take the medal from him. Foss refused.

Later, he was allowed to board the flight—with his Medal of Honor.

These were only two passenger complaints of invasion of privacy among many. Barry Steinhardt of the ACLU said, "What we are seeing is a lot of wasted energy. It's hard to justify what the purported security benefit is. We certainly should not be giving up our rights for the illusion of security."[12]

Supporters of these new screening procedures defended the screeners. They called for patience. The new security system was still a work in progress, they said. Things would get better.

They were right. Passenger complaints fell in the months and years that followed, as both screeners and passengers adjusted to these new privacy restrictions.

Superman's Vision

Terrorists target buildings that symbolize the nations they oppose. Two targets of the 9-11 attackers were the Pentagon and the White House. After the attacks, a new security system was designed to protect national monuments in and around the Washington, D.C., area. The Synchronized Operations Command Complex (SOCC) began operation in February 2002.

The operation was located in the Washington, D.C., police headquarters. In a huge room, fifty people intently watched a wall of forty video screens. The watchers controlled the zoom lenses of spycams trained on areas around the Washington Monument and other potential terrorist targets. They could zoom

In 2002, Attorney General John Ashcroft proposed Operation TIPS—Terrorist Information and Prevention System—in which citizens would report any suspicious activities they noticed. However, many objected to the idea of Americans spying on each other, so the proposal was abandoned.

in close on individuals' faces. This was important because they planned to link up with worldwide databases holding the faces of known terrorists. Then any face caught on camera could be checked against these databases to identify terrorists.

Plans also included linking up with other nearby security systems to form one vast super-surveillance network. Then the watchers at police headquarters could watch city streets and freeways. They could also look inside lobbies and elevators, subways and schools, banks and department stores, even nursing homes and hospitals.

People had mixed reactions to this new security system. Some people welcomed it. Teresa Chambers was chief of the National Park Police. She said, "Things have changed since September 11. I think the community and the public's expectation is that we will take extra measures to help protect. The cameras are part of that."[13]

On the other hand, privacy advocates were concerned. Maryland congresswoman Connie Morella said, "One of the biggest concerns that I have is that, once this system is in place, it will be too tempting for the police not to use it to its full force."[14] In other words, the police might be tempted to use the system to spy on innocent people. ACLU director of technology and liberty programs Barry Steinhardt agreed with this slippery slope argument. "Technology is giving government what amounts to Superman's vision," he said.[15]

Total Information Awareness

Now let's look at this "Superman's vision" from another angle. In addition to video surveillance, this vision involves data surveillance. Imagine that all the information about everyone in the United States has been collected, categorized, and entered into separate computer databases. One database houses all the information about driver's licenses, for instance, another about airline ticket purchases, another about visas granted to foreign visitors, and so on.

Now picture these separate sources linked into one central database. This was the ultimate objective of TIA (Total Information Awareness), a federal project designed to detect terrorists. TIA was designed by the Defense Advanced Research Projects Agency (DARPA). This was the same agency that helped to create the Internet and the stealth bomber.

The idea for TIA came shortly after the 9-11 hijackings. TIA's designers imagined a single vast database that would do what the many separate databases had failed to do: find potential terrorists. All the separate bits of information about a potential terrorist might never arouse suspicion. But when they were gathered all together into a personal profile, the suspicions would stand out. The potential terrorist would be identified.

TIA supporters said that without this system in place, terrorists stood a good chance of staying hidden. They pointed to Khalid Al-Midhar as a tragic example. Al-Midhar was one of the nineteen 9-11 hijackers. The FBI had him on their terrorist watch list. They very much wanted to get hold of him for questioning. Agents knew he was somewhere in the United States, but they did not know where.

They could have found out, though. To buy his September 11 ticket on the flight that later crashed into the World Trade Center, Al-Midhar used a credit card issued in his own name. Under TIA, databases of the FBI would have been linked with credit card databases. Then agents could have found Al-Midhar's address, apprehended him, and, perhaps, prevented the 9-11 catastrophe. Lieutenant Colonel Doug Dyer is a member of DARPA. He said, "Three thousand people died on 9/11. When you consider the potential effect of a terrorist attack against the privacy of an entire population, there has to be some trade-off."[16]

TIA and Privacy

The TIA project fueled a national debate about the need for privacy rights versus the need for safety and security. In 2003, the project's name was changed from "Total" to "Terrorist" to emphasize its true purpose of fighting terrorism. FBI agent William D. Gore said, "It smacks of Big Brother, and I understand people's concern. But somehow I'd rather have the FBI have access to this data than some telemarketer who is intent on ripping you off."[17]

When he mentioned telemarketers, Agent Gore hit on an important point in the debate. Most of the information that would go into TIA was not secret. It was already stored in separate databases available to the public. So, Gore asked, why not centralize all this public information so law enforcement agents can use it to track down terrorists?

People who opposed TIA doubted that the project could work as designed. They doubted that this vast amount of information could ever be properly organized. Lee Tien is with the Electronic Frontier Foundation. He said,

> What I don't want to see is a system that's the worst of both worlds, unable to predict acts of

terrorism in a timely manner because of the sheer mass of mostly irrelevant information clogging its channels. . . .[18]

TIA opponents also used the slippery slope argument. Computer scientist Barbara Simon said she worried about "the potential uses that this technology might be put, if not by this administration then by a future one. Once you've got it in place you can't control it."[19]

Some opponents were members of Congress. Senator Russell Feingold of Wisconsin said,

> Our current privacy laws are inadequate to deal with new techniques of data mining, which have the ability to access extensive files containing both public and private government records on each and every American. The administration should suspend not only the TIA, but all other data-mining initiatives . . . until Congress can determine whether the promised benefits come at too high a price for our privacy and personal liberties.[20]

In a November 2002 editorial, *The New York Times* agreed: "Ostensibly designed to enhance national security, it could lead to an invasion of personal privacy on a massive scale."[21]

Privacy advocates won the debate over TIA. In September 2003, the U.S. House of Representatives eliminated all money to run the program. The project was dead.

A Final Word

The privacy debate continues, with valid arguments on both sides. On the one hand, people have the right to keep their private lives to themselves, free of government interference. On the other hand, government officials must have a certain amount of freedom to look into people's private lives. Otherwise, they will not be able to effectively protect them from harm. Lawyer and civil rights activist Floyd Abrams sums up the present status of rights to privacy concisely and eloquently when he says:

> It seems to me that what occurred on Sept. 11 was a transformative act in our history. While people are trying to go back to life as it was before Sept. 11, I don't think it's possible. . . . I think we have to be prepared to pay some prices, particularly in the privacy area. But the Orwellian vision must always be in our minds.[22]

Chronology

1791—The Bill of Rights is added to the U.S. Constitution. The Fourth Amendment protects U.S. citizens from "unreasonable searches and seizures" by government authorities. Protections are limited to home and personal possessions.

1877—Lawmakers widen search-and-seizure protections to include a person's mail.

1890—The *Harvard Law Review* publishes "The Right to Privacy," about the press invading personal privacy. Authors Samuel Warren and Louis Brandeis urge courts to protect intangibles, such as thoughts, feelings, and reputation. They insist that people have "the right to be let alone." Their plea is based on the "due process" clause of the Fourteenth Amendment. More than one hundred years later, their article is still a foundation of privacy law.

1891—*Union Pacific Railway Co.* v. *Botsford*. The U.S. Supreme Court further widens privacy protections to include a person's tangible, physical self.

1949—British author George Orwell publishes *1984*. This influential science fiction novel tells of a world in which privacy is under government control. Privacy advocates often refer to the book's totalitarian leader, Big Brother, when they talk about privacy concerns.

1965—*Griswold* v. *Connecticut*. The U.S. Supreme Court establishes the concept of "zones of privacy," areas in which personal privacy is protected from government interference. These zones now include the personal lives of married couples.

1969—*Tinker* v. *Des Moines Independent School District*. For the first time, the U.S. Supreme Court addresses the constitutional rights of students. They rule that students on school grounds retain their constitutional rights of freedom of speech and expression.

1973—*Roe* v. *Wade*. The U.S. Supreme Court widens the zones of privacy to include a woman's right to decide for herself whether to terminate a pregnancy.

1974—Federal lawmakers pass the Privacy Act, forbidding government agencies from spying on American citizens who are not part of a criminal investigation. The act is a reaction to decades of illegal surveillance of some 13,000 Americans by the FBI and other secret agencies.

Federal lawmakers also pass the Family Educational Rights and Privacy Act (FERPA), setting guidelines about school records. Students, once they reach age eighteen, and their parents are guaranteed access to all student records.

1985—*New Jersey* v. *T.L.O.* For the first time in legal history, the U.S. Supreme Court states that students have legitimate expectations of privacy while on school grounds.

1993—New York becomes the first big U.S. city to install red-light cameras to discourage drivers from speeding and running red lights. Other big cities soon follow. Privacy advocates generally do not complain, since only lawbreakers are photographed.

1995—*Acton* v. *Veronia School District 47J.* The U.S. Supreme Court rules that schools may give drug tests to students who intend to play school sports.

1998—Members of the Americans Civil Liberties Union inspect New York City looking for video surveillance cameras. They find nearly 2,400 in operation.

2000—Authorities nab the notorious "Wig Bandit" bank robber when bank surveillance tapes are shown on TV and a viewer recognizes him. More criminals continue to be caught each year thanks to video surveillance tapes.

Privacy advocates expose Carnivore, an undercover FBI operation that monitors computer e-mails. Government officials assure the public that Carnivore looks at e-mails of suspected criminals only. Privacy advocates remain skeptical.

2001—Federal lawmakers pass the Patriot Act, expanding the government's powers to look into people's private lives. The act is a reaction to the terrorist attacks of September 11, 2001, and is the first major step in the U.S. war on terrorism.

2002—Federal lawmakers establish the Department of Homeland Security, combining twenty-two separate agencies. This is another reaction to the events of September 11, 2001. Privacy advocates are concerned about so much power and information concentrated in a single department.

In *Board of Education of Independent School District No. 92 of Pottawatomie County et al. v. Earls et al.*, the U.S. Supreme Court widens its ruling in *Acton*. Schools may now give drug tests to students who wish to take part in any extracurricular activities, not just sports.

Federal agents break up the largest identity theft ring to date, with an estimated 30,000 victims.

2003—The federal government's Total Information Awareness program (TIA) is renamed *Terrorist* Information Awareness. The program aims to centralize information databases on all Americans to detect terrorist activity. Opponents say TIA threatens rights to privacy. The program is abolished by Congress.

New medical privacy rules go into effect, limiting the information that hospitals, doctors, and pharmacists may give out without the patient's consent. Privacy advocates insist these protections do not go far enough.

A national do-not-call list is scheduled to go into effect, barring most telemarketers from calling people who register to have their names put on the list. But telemarketers file suit, and the matter goes to the courts for resolution.

Chapter Notes

Chapter 1. Privacy's Widening Scope

1. *Union Pacific Railway Co.* v. *Botsford 141 US 250.* Supreme Court of the United States (1891). Cited in *Cruzan* v. *Director, MDH 497 U.S. 261.* Supreme Court of the United States (1990), <http://caselaw.lp.findlaw.com/scripts/getcase.pl?court=us&vol=497&invol=261> (June 10, 2003).

2. Samuel D. Warren and Louis D. Brandeis, "The Right to Privacy," *Harvard Law Review*, December 15, 1890, <http://www.lawrence.edu/fac/boardmaw/Privacy_brand_warr2.html> (June 10, 2003).

3. Ibid.

Chapter 2. Watchers and Listeners

1. Katharine Mieszkowski, "Nowhere Left to Hide," *Salon.com*, June 18, 2001, <http://archive.salon.com/tech/feature/2001/06/18/webcam_privacy> (June 10, 2003).

2. B.J. Reyes, "Hawaiian Drivers Creative in Skirting New Speed Cameras," *Chicago Tribune*, March 6, 2002, p. 10.

3. "Close Watch," *CBSNews.com*, April 21, 2002, <http://www.cbsnews.com/stories/2002/04/19/sunday/main506739.shtml> (June 10, 2003).

Chapter 3. Searches and Seizures

1. *Payton* v. *New York No. 78-5420.* Supreme Court of the United States (1980), <http://www.uchastings.edu/bisharat_01/CrimPro%20Cases/445_us_573.htm> (June 10, 2003).

2. *Kyllo* v. *United States No. 99-8508.* Supreme Court of the United States (2001), <http://www.law.umkc.edu/faculty/projects/ftrials/conlaw/kyllo.htm> (July 14, 2003).

3. Rosemarie Bernardo, "Surveillance Cameras Pivotal in Crime Fight," *Honolulu Star-Bulletin*, April 15, 2002, <http://www.starbulletin.com/2002/04/15/news/story3.html> (July 14, 2003).

4. *Sibron* v. *New York 392 U.S. 40.* Supreme Court of the United States (1968), <http://caselaw.lp.findlaw.com/scripts/getcase.pl?court=us&vol=392&invol=40> (July 14, 2003).

5. Christopher Dreher, "Big Brother Is Watching You Read," *Salon.com*, February 13, 2002, <http://www.salon.com/books/feature/2002/02/13/bookstores/index.html?x> (June 10, 2003).

6. Michael Moss and Ford Fessenden, "New Tools for Domestic Spying, and Qualms," *New York Times*, December 10, 2002, <http://www.nytimes.com/2002/12/10/national/10PRIV.html> (June 10, 2003).

7. Christopher Newton, "Librarians Grow Uneasy as FBI Checks Records," *Chicago Sun-Times*, June 25, 2002, <http://www.suntimes.com/output/terror/cst-nws-lib25.html> (June 26, 2002).

Chapter 4. Intrusions and Exposures

1. Dorothy J. Glancy, "The Invention of the Right to Privacy," *Arizona Law Review*, vol. 21, no. 1, 1979, p. 10, <http://www.scu.edu/law/FacWebPage/Glancy/assets/images/Privacy.pdf> (June 10, 2003).

2. *Wilson et al.* v. *Layne, Deputy United States Marshal, et al. No. 98-83.* Supreme Court of the United States (1999), <http://supct.law.cornell.edu/supct/html/98-83.ZO.html> (June 10, 2003).

3. Stephen Kinzer, "In Cincinnati, Art Bows to the Privacy of Death," *New York Times*, August 3, 2002, <http://www.nytimes.com/2002/08/03/

arts/design/03MORG.html?ex=1055390400&en=
61c93d0ae5b95455&ei=5070> (June 10, 2003).

4. "Privacy," University of Montana School of
Journalism, <http://www.umt.edu/journalism/student
_resources/class_web_sites/media_law/privacy.html>
(November 14, 2002).

5. "Video Voyeurs," *techtv*, August 13, 2002,
<http://www.techtv.com/cybercrime/print/0,2310
2,3380883,00.html> (November 12, 2002).

6. Jere Longman, "Videotaped Athletes Win
Federal Lawsuit," *New York Times*, December 5,
2002, <http://www.nytimes.com/2002/12/05/
sports/othersports/05VIDE.html?ex=1055390400
&en=511fff84b5e9d3d7&ei=5070> (June 10,
2003).

7. Stephanie Armour, "Biometrics to Imprint
Job Site," *USA Today*, December 4, 2002,
<http://www.usatoday.com/money/industries/tech
nology/2002-12-04-fingerprint_x.htm> (June 10,
2003).

Chapter 5. Students: A Special Case

1. *Tinker* v. *Des Moines Independent School
District 393 U.S. 503.* Supreme Court of the United
States (1969), <http://caselaw.lp.findlaw.com/
scripts/getcase.pl?court=us&vol=393&invol=503>
(June 10, 2003).

2. *New Jersey* v. *T.L.O. 468 U.S. 1214* Supreme
Court of the United States (1984), <http:// www.
departments.bucknell.edu/edu/pa_law/Demotion/
tlo.html> (June 10, 2003).

3. Ibid.

4. Ellen Alderman and Caroline Kennedy, *The
Right to Privacy* (New York: Knopf, 1995), p. 46.

5. *Board of Education of Independent School
District No. 92 of Pottawatomie County et al.* v. *Earls
et al. No. 01-332.* Supreme Court of the United States
(2002), <http://caselaw.lp.findlaw.com/scripts/

getcase.pl?court=us&vol=000&invol=01-332>
(June 10, 2003).

6. Tamar Lewin, "With Court Nod, Parents Debate School Drug Tests," *New York Times*, September 29, 2002, <http://www.nytimes.com/2002/09/29/national/29DRUG.html?ex=10 55390400&en=cfdc85f036e3a33f&ei=5070> (June 10, 2003).

Chapter 6. Privacy for Sale

1. Toby Lester, "The Reinvention of Privacy," *Atlantic Online*, March 2001, <http://www.theatlantic.com/issues/2001/03/lester-p3.htm> (June 10, 2003).

2. "'Do-Not-Call' Still a Big Hit," *CBSNews.com*, July 1, 2003, <http://www.cbsnews.com/stories/2003/03/11/politics/main543573.shtml> (July 14, 2003.

3. Yochi J. Dreazen, "The Best Way To Guard Your Privacy," *Wall Street Journal*, November 18, 2002, p. R4.

4. Ibid.

5. Ann Bartow, "Our Data, Ourselves: Privacy, Propertization, and Gender," 34 U.S.F.L. Rev. 633 (Summer 2000). Quoted in "Gender and Electronic Privacy," Electronic Privacy Information Center, <http://www.epic.org/privacy/gender> (June 10, 2003).

6. Ellen Alderman and Caroline Kennedy, *The Right to Privacy* (New York: Knopf, 1995), p. 326.

7. Simson Garfinkle, *Database Nation: The Death of Privacy in the 21st Century* (Sebastopol, Calif.: O'Reilly & Associates, Inc., 2000), p. 126.

8. Donna E. Shalala, "A Loss to Medical Privacy," *New York Times*, March 30, 2002, <http://www.truthout.org/docs_02/03.31F.DS.Loss.htm> (June 10, 2003).

9. Sarah Lueck, "Tough New Law Helps Guard Patient Privacy," *Wall Street Journal*, March 19, 2003, p. D1.

Chapter 7. Privacy Stolen

1. "Testimony from Dallas, Texas: It All Started at the Supermarket," Privacy Rights Clearinghouse, October 2000, <http://www.privacyrights.org/victim15.htm> (June 10, 2003).

2. Andrea L. Foster, "ID Theft Turns Students Into Privacy Activists," *Chronicle of Higher Education*, August 2, 2002, <http://chronicle.com/free/v48/i47/47a02701.htm> (June 10, 2003).

3. Robert O'Harrow, Jr., "Rights Groups Oppose ID Card," *Washington Post*, February 13, 2002, p. A15.

4. Robert O'Harrow, Jr., "A Deadly Collection of Information," *Washington Post*, January 4, 2002, p. E01.

5. "Privacy Initiatives," Federal Trade Commission, n.d., <http://www.ftc.gov/privacy/index.html> (June 10, 2003).

Chapter 8. Privacy and Terrorism

1. Michael Moss and Ford Fessenden, "New Tools for Domestic Spying, and Qualms," *New York Times*, December 10, 2002, <http://www.nytimes.com/2002/12/10/national/10PRIV.html> (June 10, 2003).

2. Kevin Curran, "War on Terror Worries Privacy Advocates," *NewsMax.com*, October 31, 2001, <http://newsmax.com/archives/articles/2001/10/30/162113.shtml> (June 10, 2003).

3. Adam Liptak, "F.B.I. Faces No Legal Obstacles to Domestic Spying," *New York Times*, May 31, 2002, <http://www.truthout.org/docs_02/06.01C.fbi.ok.2.spy.htm> (June 10, 2003).

4. Moss and Fessenden.

5. Dean Reynolds, "Difficult Equation," *ABCNews.com*, May 31, 2002, <http://abcnews.go.com/sections/wnt/DailyNews/fbipowers020530.html> (June 10, 2003).

6. Ibid.

7. "DHS Organization: Building a Secure Homeland," U.S. Department of Homeland Security, n.d., <http://www.dhs.gov/dhspublic/theme_home1.jsp> (June 10, 2003).

8. Tom Ridge, "Remarks by Homeland Security Director Tom Ridge to the National Association of Broadcasters Education Foundation 2002 Service to America Summit," June 10, 2002, <http://www.whitehouse.gov/news/releases/2002/06/2002061 0-7.html> (June 10, 2003).

9. Andy Newman, "Citizen Snoops Wanted," *New York Times*, July 21, 2002, <http://www.nytimes.com/2002/07/21/weekinreview/21NEWM.html> (June 10, 2003).

10. Joan Biskupic, "Attention Turns Back to Liberties," *USA Today*, October 31, 2002, <http://www.usatoday.com/news/politicselections/2002-10-31-liberties-usat_x.htm> (June 10, 2003).

11. Dahlia Lithwick, "A Snitch in Time," *Slate*, July 31, 2002, <http://slate.msn.com/?id=2068690> (June 10, 2003).

12. "Public's Anger Simmers Over Airport Searches," *Holland Sentinel*, March 11, 2002, <http://www.hollandsentinel.com/stories/031102/new_031102005.shtml> (June 10, 2003).

13. "Close Watch," *CBSNews.com*, April 21, 2002, <http://www.cbsnews.com/stories/2002/04/19/sunday/main506739.shtml> (June 10, 2003).

14. Ibid.

15. Jess Bravin, "Washington Police to Play 'I Spy,'" *Wall Street Journal*, February 13, 2002, p. B1.

16. Aaron Ricadela, "Total Information Awareness Project Undergoes First Test," *InformationWeek*, April 10, 2003, <http://www.financetech.com/story/techwire/IWK20030410S0018> (June 10, 2003).

17. Moss and Fessenden.

18. Eliot Borin, "Feds Open 'Total' Tech Spy System," *Wired News*, August 7, 2002, <http://www.wired.com/news/print/0,1294,54342,00.html> (June 10, 2003).

19. John Markoff, "Pentagon Plans a Computer System that Would Peek at Personal Data of Americans," *New York Times*, November 9, 2002, <http://www.nytimes.com/2002/11/09/politics/09COMP.html?ex=1055390400&en=c3e2dd6a881189d6&ei=5070> (June 10, 2003).

20. Adam Clymer, "New Name of Pentagon Data Sweep Focuses on Terror," *New York Times*, May 21, 2003, <http://www.nytimes.com/2003/05/21/international/worldspecial/21PRIV.html> (June 10, 2003).

21. "A Snooper's Dream," *New York Times*, November 18, 2002, <http://www.nytimes.com/2002/11/18/opinion/18MON1.html?ex=1055390400&en=25ed7b796a6c1319&ei=5070> (June 10, 2003).

22. David Wallis, "Questions for Floyd Abrams: Fighting With the Right," *New York Times Magazine*, April 7, 2002, p. 17.

Glossary

American Civil Liberties Union (ACLU)—A national nonprofit organization dedicated to defending and preserving the individual rights and liberties guaranteed by the Constitution and laws of the United States. The ACLU works to preserve rights of privacy.

Big Brother—In George Orwell's science fiction novel *1984*, the authority figure in a totalitarian society where personal privacy is nonexistent. It is widely used when referring to actions of the federal government that threaten privacy.

bright line ruling—A legal ruling that makes clear distinctions or draws clear boundaries. In privacy matters, the courts draw a "bright line" at the doorstep of a home, making the home a zone of privacy.

Carnivore—A secret FBI eavesdropping operation in which e-mails of suspected criminals are monitored by federal agents, using software installed on Internet servers.

cookies—Invisible electronic markers attached to a person's computer that allow Internet companies to record the Web sites that a person visits.

credit report—Detailed information on a person's credit history, including credit card accounts, loans, and any late payments. Lenders consult it when deciding whether to lend a person money.

due process clause—A clause in the Fourteenth Amendment to the Constitution that guarantees that authorities must use proper legal procedures. In privacy matters, due process often affects searches and seizures.

exclusionary rule—A rule that prevents prosecutors from introducing illegally obtained evidence at a trial. In privacy matters, the exclusionary rule often relates to evidence obtained during a search.

intrusion tort—A tort that involves invasion of privacy, with one party intruding upon the solitude of another in a highly offensive manner. Many intrusion cases involve members of the press covering stories and law enforcement officers serving warrants.

Patriot Act—Act of Congress passed in October 2001 in response to the September 11 terrorist attacks. The act amends some federal statutes involving privacy, giving government agents greater powers of surveillance in regard to suspected terrorists.

pretexting—Deceptive practices investigators use to pry private information about a person from that person's friends, coworkers, or family members.

privacy—People's need to be let alone and to control who knows what about them. Privacy can be invaded both legally and illegally. Illegal invasions of privacy violate rights guaranteed in the Constitution.

private facts tort—A tort that involves invasion of privacy, with one party publishing facts that, while true, are highly offensive to another party.

Private facts cases often focus on the press's First Amendment right to freely publish the news.

probable cause—A reasonable belief that a person has committed a crime. The Fourth and Fourteenth Amendments forbid law officers from arresting persons without probable cause.

reasonable in scope standard—A standard for searches of students by school officials on school grounds. When searching, officials must use reasonable measures and avoid being excessively intrusive.

reasonable suspicion standard—A standard for searches of students by school officials on school grounds. Before searching, officials must have reasonable grounds for suspecting that their search will turn up evidence of wrongdoing.

search and seizure clause—In the Fourth Amendment to the Constitution, a clause that protects people from having their property searched or taken by state or federal authorities who are conducting a criminal investigation.

search warrant—An official order authorizing a search of someone's home or other personal property. Most searches require that authorities first get a warrant from a judge, showing that they have reason to believe that criminal activity is involved.

slippery slope argument—The argument that a proposal is dangerous because, if put into action, it will lead to a series of increasingly negative events. Privacy advocates apply this argument when speaking against extending government surveillance powers.

spam—Electronic junk mail that pops up or under Web pages or is sent to e-mail inboxes.

surveillance—The act of keeping watch over persons or places in order to gather information. Electronic technology threatens privacy because of its surveillance capabilities.

telemarketer—A person trying to sell products or services by telephone, making large volumes of unsolicited calls. Telemarketers are bound by law not to call people whose names appear on a do-not-call list.

torts—Legal disputes between private individuals or organizations. In a tort, a victim (the plaintiff) generally seeks money from a person or corporation who harmed him or her (the defendant). Many tort cases involve claims of invasion of privacy.

Total Information Awareness/Terrorist Information Awareness (TIA)—A project meant to help federal agencies track down terrorists by sharing vast amounts of computerized information about American citizens and aliens. Privacy advocates claim that TIA is a serious threat to privacy.

voyeur—A person who secretly spies on another person, often using miniature wireless video cameras or eavesdropping equipment. In certain instances, voyeurs may be punished by law.

Further Reading

Bridegam, Martha. *The Right to Privacy*. Philadelphia: Chelsea House, 2002.

DeAngelis, Gina. *Cybercrimes*. Philadelphia: Chelsea House, 2002.

Henderson, Harry. *Privacy in the Information Age*. New York: Facts on File, 1999.

Hyatt, Michael. *Invasion of Privacy: How to Protect Yourself in the Digital Age*. Washington, D.C.: Regnery, 2001.

Jacobs, Thomas. *Teens on Trial: Young People Who Challenged the Law—and Changed Your Life*. Minneapolis, Minn.: Free Spirit, 2000.

McGwire, Scarlett. *Surveillance: The Impact on Our Lives*. Austin, Tex.: Raintree Steck-Vaughn, 2001.

Internet Addresses

Privacy.Org

<http://www.privacy.org>

Electronic Privacy Information Center

<http://www.epic.org/privacy>

Identity Theft

<http://www.consumer.gov/idtheft>

Index

A

Abrams, Floyd, 107
airport searches, 100–101
Alderman, Ellen, 74
American Civil Liberties
    Union (ACLU), 21, 25,
    47, 97, 101, 103
America's Most Wanted, 22, 24
Armey, Dick, 99
Ashcroft, John, 98–99
Augafa, Felix, 34

B

Bartow, Ann, 73
Big Brother, 19–22, 83,
    94, 105
Bill of Rights, 9–10, 13, 97
bookstores, 38
Brandeis, Louis D., 12–14, 21
Brando, Marlon, 40
bright line ruling, 42
Bush, George W., 82, 83

C

Carnivore, 27–29
Central Intelligence Agency
    (CIA), 17, 19, 97
Chambers, Teresa, 103
civil rights movement, 17
Cohen, David, 95
Colatosti, Tom, 22
Condon, Thomas, 44–45
consumer profiles, 66–67, 74
cookies, 71
Cottrell, Lance, 70–71

court cases
    Acton v. *Veronia School
        District 47J*, 61–62
    *Board of Education of
        Independent School
        District No. 92 of
    Desnick* v. *ABC*, 41–42
    Griswold v. *Connecticut*, 15
    Hanlon v. *Berger*, 42
    Kyllo v. *United States*,
        31–33, 34
    New Jersey v. *T.L.O.*,
        52–54, 56, 57
    Pottawatomie County et al.
        v. *Earls et al.*, 62
    Roe v. *Wade*, 15
    Sibron v. *New York*, 35
    Sipple v. *Chronicle
        Publishing Co.*, 45–46
    Tinker v. *Des Moines
        Independent School
        District*, 52
    Union Pacific Railway Co.
        v. *Botsford*, 11–12, 41
    U.S. v. *Drayton*, 36, 40
    Widener v. *Frye*, 55–56
    Wilson v. *Layne*, 42
credit cards, 7, 66, 79–81,
    90–91, 104
credit reports, 81

D

Defense Advanced Research
    Projects Agency
    (DARPA), 104

Department of Homeland
  Security (DHS), 97–98
direct mail, 67, 90
do-not-call list, 69–70
Drug Enforcement
  Administration (DEA),
  36–37
drug testing, 59–62, 64
due process clause, 14–15
Dyer, Doug, 105

E
Eastman, George, 13
Einstein, Albert, 17
Electronic Privacy Information
  Center (EPIC), 28
e-mail, 27–29, 71–72, 91–92
exclusionary rule, 32–33, 57

F
Family Educational Rights and
  Privacy Act of 1974
  (FERPA), 58–59
Federal Bureau of Investigation
  (FBI), 17, 19, 27–28, 95,
  97, 104, 105
Federal Trade Commission
  (FTC), 69–70, 88, 94
Feingold, Russell, 106
First Amendment, 40, 45,
  50, 95
Fortas, Abe, 52
Foss, Joe, 100–101
Fourteenth Amendment, 14, 15
Fourth Amendment, 10, 15,
  16, 30–31, 33, 34,
  42, 61
freedom of speech, 40, 45,
  50, 52
freedom of the press, 39–43,
  45–46

G
Gallela, Ron, 40, 41
Gatewood, Stanton, 81

Geoffino, Tom, 38
Gore, William D., 105

H
Hanson, Kari, 38
Hatch, Orrin, 99
Health Insurance Portability
  and Accountability Act
  (HIPAA), 77
Horsley, Neal, 50

I
identity theft, 78–83
in loco parentis, 51–52
Internet, 28, 47, 48, 50, 66,
  70–73, 79, 84–85,
  90–92
intrusion tort, 41–44

J
junk mail, *see* direct mail

K
Kennedy, Caroline, 74
King, Martin Luther, 17

L
libraries, 38
Lindley, Michael, 64
lockers, 56, 57–58, 64

M
McNealy, Scott, 71
medical records,
  74–77
Meskis, Joyce, 37–38
metal detectors, 57
Morella, Connie, 103
Mueller, Robert, 97
Murphy, Laura, 97

N
Nadel, Norbert, 45
Nader, Ralph, 43–44
national identity cards,
  81–83

O

O'Connor, Sandra Day, 61
Orwell, George, 20–22,
    99, 107

P

Patriot Act of 2001, 18–19,
    38, 95, 97–98
Pitofsky, Robert, 94
pretexting, 85–86
privacy
    of students, 51–62, 64
    protecting, 88–92
    zones of, 14–15, 31–34,
        36, 47
Privacy Act of 1974, 17–19
private facts tort, 45–46
probable cause, 11, 35,
    53–54
public records, 73–74

R

reasonable in scope standard,
    54–56, 57
reasonable suspicion stan-
    dard, 54, 56–58
Rehnquist, William, 42
Ridge, Tom, 98
Rotenberg, Marc, 28
Rucireto, Richard, 99
Ryder, Winona, 24

S

Scalia, Antonin, 32, 61
Schaeffer, Rebecca, 84
Scott, Kenneth, 50
searches and seizures, 10, 16,
    30–38, 53–58, 61, 85
September 11, 2001, 18, 38,
    82, 93–94, 99–101,
    104–105, 107

Shalala, Donna, 75–76
Simon, Barbara, 106
slippery slope argument, 25,
    27, 103, 106
Social Security numbers,
    78–81, 89
spam, 71–73, 91
stalking, 84–86
Steinhardt, Barry, 47–48,
    101, 103
Stevens, John Paul, 31
student records, 58–59
student rights, 51–62, 64

T

telemarketing, 67, 69–70, 91
terrorism, 18–19, 29, 38,
    82, 93–95, 97–107
Terrorist Information and
    Prevention System (TIPS),
    98–99
Thomas, Clarence, 62
Tien, Lee, 105–106
Tobias, Jonathan, 44–45
torts, 41, 44–46
Total/Terrorist Information
    Awareness (TIA), 103–106

V

Velázquez, Nydia, 75
video surveillance cameras,
    21–22, 24–25, 29, 34,
    46–48, 50, 101–103
voyeurism, 46–47

W

Warren, Earl, 35
Warren, Samuel D.,
    12–14, 21
Westin, Alan, 65
White, Mary Jo, 94